Dancing

with a

Shadow

W9-BZV-840

Discovery House PUBLISHERS

BOX 3566 · GRAND RAPIDS, MI 49501

*PUBLISHING BOOKS THAT FEED
THE SOUL WITH THE WORD OF GOD.*

Dancing
with a
Shadow

Making Sense of God's Silence

Daniel Schaeffer

Dedication

I dedicate this book to the one who encouraged me to write it.
My friend, companion, supporter, lover, and mother of my children, my wife,
Annette.
Without her this book would not have been possible.

You do so much, and ask so little. This, at least, is for you alone.

Dancing With A Shadow
Copyright © 1995 by Daniel A. Schaeffer

Discovery House Publishers is affiliated with
RBC Ministries, Grand Rapids, Michigan 49512

Discovery House books are distributed to the trade by
Thomas Nelson Publishers, Nashville, Tennessee 37214

All Scripture quotations are from the
New American Standard Bible.
Copyright © 1960, 1962, 1968, 1971, 1972
The Lockman Foundation. Used by permission.

Library of Congress Cataloging-in-Publication Data

Schaeffer, Daniel A.
    Dancing with a shadow: making sense of God's silence /
Daniel A. Schaeffer.
        p.   cm.

    ISBN 0-929239-73-3

    1. Bible. O.T. Esther—Criticism, interpretation, etc.
2. Providence and government of God. I. Title.
BS1375.2.S32   1995
222'.906—dc20   94-43711
                                            CIP

All rights reserved.

Printed in the United States of America

95 96 97 98 99 / CHG / 10 9 8 7 6 5 4 3 2 1

Contents

As the Curtain Opens

One of our favorite family vacations is camping in Yosemite National Park, in the High Sierras of California. We have gone every year since my wife and I were married. Our kids enjoy it too, especially sleeping in a tent under a canopy of stars.

It was on one such trip several years ago, when the sun began to fade, that we decided to make a quick trip to the local general store for marshmallows. An evening under the majestic trees and beside the awesome mountains was never considered complete until we had roasted marshmallows by campfire.

But it was pitch black when we arrived back from the store, so I led our wary band of young pioneers carefully and slowly through the darkness to our picnic table and lantern. Christi, then five years old, Andrew, our three-year-old, and Katie, our two-year-old, sat quietly on the picnic table as I fumbled with the matches.

I had just lit the lantern when my son suddenly yelled out in a terrified voice, "Monster!" and pointed behind me. I quickly turned around, and sure enough, there against the backdrop of some large trees was a huge shadow that loomed some fifty feet high. For a moment, even I was unnerved, as I looked quickly for its source. But as I leaned forward to get a better look, the shadow suddenly moved with me. I instantly realized we were looking at my shadow.

The lantern behind me had projected my shadow up against the wall of trees and had made it huge. I quickly explained this to my frightened children and then moved them closer to the light where we spent some delightful moments dancing with our shadows. It was only later that I reflected upon that moment.

The shadow on the tree was simply a reflection of my presence. Looking at my shadow would not reveal anything specific about me. You couldn't look at my shadow and then describe me with any detail. My age, height, the color of my eyes, my hair, and the expression on my face would all be mysteries. The only thing you would know for certain was that the shadow reflected the presence of someone.

The more I thought about that the more I realized how much my life reflected that truth. Someone once said, "God is a lot like my pastor, I don't see him during the week, and I don't understand him on Sunday!" There have been many frightening moments in my life when I sought desperately to pinpoint God's activities and whereabouts, but each time all I saw was His shadow.

I identified with the words of Sir Robert Anderson.

"A silent heaven is the greatest mystery of our existence." Some there are, indeed, for whom the problem has no perplexities. In a philosophy of silly optimism, or a life of selfish isolation, they have "attained Nirvana." For such the sad and hideous realities of life around us have no existence. Upon their path these cast no shadow. The serene atmosphere of their fools' paradise is undisturbed by the cry of the suffering and the oppressed. But earnest and thoughtful men face these realities, and have ears to hear that cry; and their indignant wonder finds utterance at times in some such words as those of the old Hebrew prophet and bard, "Doth God know? And is there knowledge in the Most High?"[1]

That's why it is sometimes hard to read stories in the Bible about God speaking from a burning bush, or through thunder, or miraculously leading the children of Israel through the desert with a pillar of cloud by day, and a pillar of fire by night.

We witness how God's people were delivered in such supernatural ways: plagues of locusts upon their enemies, the parting of the Red Sea, manna raining down from heaven. In many cases God intervened in direct and miraculous ways in the crisis points of their lives. It can be difficult to read about those incredible events happening and then not get a little discouraged by the fact that He never reacts that way to us in the crisis points of *our* lives.

I believe wholeheartedly in the truth of Scripture, and yet the God in these Scriptures, the One who divided the

---

1. Sir Robert Anderson, *The Silence of God.* Grand Rapids: Kregel, 1978, 1.

sea and devastated evil armies and intervened in times of distress, seemed far removed from my experiences. The evil people I knew never seemed to get what was coming to them. In fact, at times I wondered if *I* wasn't getting what was coming to them.

It is the silence of heaven that causes the most frustration. We know God can communicate, but we are at a loss to know why He doesn't choose to. And when we don't hear from Him, we wonder if He's there, or if He's paying attention to what's going on down here.

Be honest—aren't there times in your life when you would like to see God's direct intervention? A telegram from God informing you of who you are to marry, or what your vocation should be, or how you are ever going to get out of your present predicament would be truly welcome, but none of us are holding our breath.

And sometimes we feel cheated, because isn't that the way God is *supposed* to work? Isn't He in the miracle business? Sometimes it seems as if God has closed up shop and hung out the "Gone Fishing" sign just when we need Him most.

But before we start attempting to make excuses for our God, we should know that He was very aware that we would struggle with this issue. And knowing beforehand that we would face this confusion, He provided a very special book in the Old Testament. This book is called Esther, named after its main character.

The precious value of the book of Esther is that it is a book of crisis—something we can relate to—and it provides the answers to what God is doing when He chooses to remain silent! From beginning to end the purpose of this book is to demonstrate the providential care of God over His people. The key word is *providential*.

Providence comes from the Latin *provideo*, which means "to see a thing beforehand." Esther is a case study of the way God *normally* and *ordinarily* works on our behalf.

One man aptly described God's activity in Esther.

> He may be invisible, but He is infallible. He may seem strangely silent, but He remains actively sovereign. He may be unsuspected; yet omnisciently, omnipresently, omnipotently, He guides and guards. Evil may be temporarily permitted, but ultimately it is frustrated. Behind a frowning providence God hides a smiling face.[2]

Throughout the entire book of Esther God stands silently in the shadows choosing not to intervene supernaturally, yet carefully, providentially working out His will.

When we don't see miracles, and we don't sense or feel the presence of God, we are apt to say, "He's not watching; He's not caring; He's not involved." But Esther shouts out the truth that God is *vitally* involved in the affairs of our lives, and He is actively working on our behalf.

I know that this can seem hard to believe at times. All my life I have struggled to make sense of God's silence and His apparent inactivity when it seemed I needed Him most.

But the answer came at a most inauspicious moment. One day, as I was sitting in my office deciding which book of the Bible to preach through next, I flipped through the pages of the Old Testament and my eyes fastened on a verse in this obscure book called Esther.

---

2. J. Sidlow Baxter, *Explore the Book.* Grand Rapids: Zondervan, 1966, 264.

Though I had six years of seminary training under my belt, I wasn't well acquainted with this book, and it seemed an unlikely candidate for a series. Honestly, I would have kept leafing through the pages but for the words of that one verse I spied.

For if you remain silent at this time, relief and deliverance will arise for the Jews from another place and you and your father's house will perish. And who knows whether you have not attained royalty for such a time as this? (Esther 4:14)

These words, though separated from any context I was aware of, seemed to hint at an answer to a gnawing question I had always struggled with. While I still had absolutely no intention of preaching on this book, I felt compelled to make sense of that little verse.

So to satisfy curiosity I went to the beginning of the book and read it through in one sitting. As I did, I got excited, like a collector stumbling upon an antique of immense value with a price tag of fifty cents.

I simply couldn't put it down—mulling it over and over again, each time seeing more than I did before. Before long I did decide to preach through this little book, but admittedly more for my own sake than for my congregation's benefit.

So as you read this book, realize it is not an attempt at a commentary, nor a verse by verse exposition, both of which have been successfully accomplished by others far more qualified than I. It is rather a deeper look at the silence of God in a book designed to give us a peek behind the thin veil that separates this world from the heavenly realm. It offers us a glimpse of how God works in the ordinary affairs of human beings without the blatantly divine interventions we often seek.

Esther has been properly called a drama. It is all that and more. For that reason all my chapters reflect the theme of the stage and a theatrical production, for it was on this grand historical stage that God revealed for Dan Schaeffer, and anyone else who would listen, His divine modus operandi.

It is my prayer that you will begin to discern the behind-the-scenes work of God in your own life and realize how frequently you have danced with His shadow. Maybe then His silence will make more sense.

In fact, it may well be that you will discover, as I did, that these truths are more than theoretical pretense in your life. For it was during a quiet time in my life, when things seemed blissfully routine and under control, that I received news that would wrench these truths from my clean and sterile academic world and thrust them into the messy world of hard reality.

One

Dancing with a Shadow

Theirs seemed the ideal Christian family. He was a young and dynamic pastor who had taken an older church in decline and seen it grow dramatically under his leadership. His wife was a lovely Christian woman, the granddaughter of missionaries to China, his companion and best friend. Their marriage was strong, and their home was a delight.

They had two children, a son and a daughter, with a third due any day. Things couldn't get much better. The baby finally arrived, a beautiful and healthy little girl. The delivery went smoothly and without complications, until the fateful day they were to check out of the hospital.

Earlier that morning the wife began to experience abdominal pain, pain that increased in severity throughout the day. She had contracted a type-A strep infection, the same kind that killed Jim Henson, creator of the Muppets. She immediately went into septic shock, and by nightfall she was losing the fight for her life.

They are our best friends; in fact, we had been on vacation with them only a few weeks earlier. When we heard the news, my wife and I rushed to be with them. Two days after she fell ill we met him in the hospital.

He wasn't the same man we had left a few weeks earlier. The confident, always joking man we had come to know so well over the many years of our friendship had changed. He hadn't slept in two days, and probably hadn't eaten either. He shared bluntly, almost numbly, that the doctors had told him her chances of survival were slim. Her heart had almost failed, her kidneys had shut down, and her white blood cell count was dangerously low. There were so many things wrong with her by this time he couldn't keep track of them all.

She lay unconscious in the intensive care unit when we arrived, a situation that was to continue for nine long weeks. Unable to do anything for her at the moment, and seeing how drained and exhausted he was, we managed to coax him into a nearby restaurant.

He resembled a prize fighter who had been caught blindside. He was dazed. His life would be transformed in a moment from a pleasant, quiet life to two straight months of fragile hopes, sleeping in hospital waiting rooms, and moment-by-moment fears.

We stayed a week before reluctantly returning home. My wife would visit again to watch their children, and we would get constant reports, most of them depressing, as the woman teetered on the edge of death, and her husband on the brink of despair. The prayers of literally hundreds of people and many churches were lifted up on her behalf, and yet, time after time she drew near to death.

It had been only about a month since I had studied and preached through Esther, learning the way that God moves silently behind the scenes in our lives. These truths were to reassure me many times during these desperate several months. I saw God's shadow as He moved in the background of their lives and ours, and it left a permanent imprint on me.

Today, the crisis is over. The wife should have died four different times, and yet she lived. But there were no dramatic miracles. Every time she was close to death her body began to work in the way it needed to, but never until the last moment, never until every medical option had been tried, and had failed.

God never worked a spectacular or dramatic miracle, and yet after every crisis I could see evidence of His shadow dancing in the background. God was working in her body the way He often works in our lives, invisibly, but surely. It gave me a confident comfort and assurance that He was completely in control.

God returned the woman to her husband and their children, and He renewed the whole family's lease on life.

In reflection I realized that at each and every turn we faced a crisis, but never for a moment did God. Many times death and loss loomed before us like the approach of night, but it was never to come. Her seemingly tenuous physical hold on life was actually as secure as my healthy one. Not for a moment was she in danger of death, from God's vantage point. God never had a crisis, *we* did!

During this whole time I also witnessed God orchestrate incredible changes in the lives of hundreds of people as they put aside their own concerns and put this one woman at the forefront of their prayer lives and of their thoughts.

This is real life, and this is what the book of Esther is all about: how God works His will in the normal course of our real lives—silently, in the shadows.

Real life

I have to be honest with you, however; never once did I, or anyone else, receive any special communiqués on her condition. It wasn't that they wouldn't have been appreciated, or wanted; they just never came. What medical steps should be taken next? Which medicines should be used? Would she survive? What do we tell the children? Would she ever be normal again? We were never told.

We've all heard the flashy out-of-town speakers with their incredible tales of God speaking to them in some miraculous but mystical fashion, and how that message changed their lives. Then we've all gone home, our faith fully charged up, full of anticipation, confident that God would speak to us that way about our present crises.

So, praying more fervently than ever, we eagerly waited for a response we could recognize—any response—but nothing came. Nothing but silence. There must be something wrong with our spiritual receivers, or our faith must be tuned to the wrong channel, we concluded sadly.

We are destined, it seems, to have to deal with the silence of God, stumbling blindly around, victims of fate, unable to receive any specific messages from God about our lives.

So when we open the pages of Esther and read about God's incredible deliverance of Esther, Mordecai, and millions of Jews living in captivity, we are startled to discover that something terribly important is missing.

Every other book in the Bible contains the one thing Esther lacks, and yet, in the end, the results are all the same. God's people are delivered, faith is honored, and heroes are made, all without the one thing we have come to expect. How in the world could we have a book of the Bible with:

No Mention of God

Strange as that may sound, it's true! The name of God is never mentioned, nor referred to. In fact Martin Luther, in a momentary lapse of self-restraint, went so far as to say that he wished the book did not exist! He could not understand the purpose of a book that neither mentioned God, nor had Him speak.

Yet in spite of this glaring omission, we can see God's obvious, undeniable activity. Ah, finally, some folks in the Bible we can relate to! This situation deserves a second look.

God gave us this unique book to show us how, without violating human free will, and without interrupting the ordinary ongoing of human affairs, He stands in the shadows of our lives, silently orchestrating everything. Nothing that occurs in our lives catches Him by surprise.

Anticipating beforehand the crises in our lives, God has already planned our deliverance through seemingly unconnected and unimportant events. God has never needed to use miracles. He *chooses* to occasionally, but He never *needs* to. Miracles are for our benefit, not His!

There are times in our lives when God does not shout His presence to us, and His silence is frustrating. As a result *we often interpret the silence of God as an indication of the absence of God.* Because we cannot see Him, cannot hear Him, do not feel His presence, and do not see Him working, we feel abandoned. We can make no sense of His silence.

Seeing God's shadow

When I was about twelve years old, my family took a vacation in a small private plane. But during the flight, we got lost over the Gulf of Mexico, and were unable to find land. Low on fuel, and in the middle of a terrible storm that tossed our little plane around like a paper airplane, I desperately prayed for deliverance, but God didn't answer.

The plane's fuel supply just kept getting lower and lower, and I faced the prospect of death for the first time. Then, at the last moment, we spied land, and half an hour later flew into the only airport within our reach. Five minutes later it closed due to poor visibility. *And I saw His shadow!* I came to realize this event had not caught Him by surprise. He had planned for our crisis long before it had ever occurred in ways we could never have foreseen or imagined.

When I was sixteen years old, I returned home from church one Sunday morning to find a police car parked in our driveway. With my heart pounding, I ran inside to find my grandparents speaking frantically to an officer who was using our phone. He was attempting to coordinate the search for my mother. She had been depressed and despondent, and had suddenly vanished.

She was finally located, but by then had taken an overdose of sleeping pills in an attempt to end her life. The paramedics who arrived on the scene discovered she wasn't breathing and had no heartbeat. I had prayed fervently for her life, but then the officer said quietly to my grandmother, "I'm sorry, your daughter has passed away." In a moment my world fell apart, and God seemed far away.

Why me? I screamed in my mind. *Why her? Why now?* Our home had already been broken, life was already difficult and filled with stress and turmoil. And now this. I felt like I couldn't take any more.

Anger turned quickly to rage, as I kicked a piece of furniture violently, sending it flying. Then I felt empty—an emptiness so deep that I can still remember it.

Just an hour before, I had sung the praises of God and His power and love, and now I had to face . . . what, I didn't know. The house was filled with the sound of wails and cries of horror and pain of a mother and a father losing their daughter, of a son and a daughter losing their mother.

But then, a few moments later, that same policeman excitedly announced over the loud crying and grieving, "They've found a heartbeat!" My heart jumped to my throat, and I felt tears of another kind. Instantly the entire household was on its knees praying with every ounce of strength it had left. With God, I had been taught, there is always hope.

We rushed to the hospital where she had been taken, and several days later we were able to talk to her. She was weak and sick, but alive and coherent! *Again I saw His shadow!* And I came to realize He had been there all the time. Her state of mind and purposes had not caught Him by surprise. He had planned her deliverance before she had planned her destruction. Even the time of our death is under His control.

As a young man I found the girl I was sure I wanted to marry. It was clear to me that God had tailor-made her just for me. I worshiped her, all the time certain she would be my life's partner. But then I discovered that she was interested in someone else, and when I cried out to God, He seemed withdrawn and silent.

Then, after several difficult, silence-filled years, I met Annette, *and I saw His shadow!* I realized He had been preparing us both all that time, working out all the circumstances to bring us together. God had been actively drawing her life and mine together, but I could never have seen it.

It is only as I have grown in my understanding of God and of how He works that I have come to realize I have been dancing with His shadow all my life. There has never been a time when He was not vitally interested and involved in my life, orchestrating circumstances and events providentially.

Reading between the lines

Now while we say that in the book of Esther there is no mention of God, in a beautifully subtle way God does make His presence known. As if to reinforce the truth that God is in the shadows watching, caring for His children, the name of God occurs in a hidden way in the original Hebrew.

The name *Yahweh,* "Lord," is secretly hidden four times in an acrostic form in several ancient manuscripts of the book of Esther, and the name *Ehyeh,* "I AM WHO I AM," once. The acrostic consonants that represent the name are written larger, to make them stand out, as though we might write it in English, YaHWeH. There are no other acrostics in the entire book, which helps to confirm the intentional purpose of these.

We may not see His name, but His handiwork is plain. Like a great wind He is invisible, but evidence of His presence and activity is everywhere.

But that is not the only fascinating aspect of Esther, because we notice another glaring omission:

No Mention of Miracles

There are no supernatural acts of God recorded in the book of Esther; yet, wonderful deliverance is brought to the Jews in order to avert what would have become a horrible massacre of millions of people. Everything that happens appears to be the outworking of circumstances in their natural sequence. In other words, *nothing supernatural occurs, but what ultimately occurs is a miracle.*

This is what makes the book so relevant to us, because I'll guess that most of us probably can't point to even one bonafide miracle in our lives. This is why Esther is so special. God's working in the lives of Esther and Mordecai is in many ways a blueprint for how He works in ours. We learn that *He* may be out of *our* sight, but *we* are never out of *His.*

My story, His shadow

Each of us has probably experienced a situation in our lives where if we think about it, God has worked a miracle out of very ordinary situations.

I come from a broken home; divorce is part of my background. Every male husband/father figure I had was poor to awful. From physical abuse to emotional abuse, I witnessed it all, and for long periods of time during those impressionable early years.

Statistically, I should have become an absentee father, devoted to everything but my family, and a distant uncommunicative husband, prone to bursts of anger and uncontrollable temper. However, none of those things has happened. And I want to be quick to point out that this had nothing to do with any unnatural abilities or strength of character on my part.

No, I was well on my way to fulfilling these statistics, with dangerous personality traits becoming more and more obvious. But along the way God brought into my young life an engineer from McDonnell Douglas, Gene Lacy, who was the sponsor of a high school youth group I started attending.

God brought this man along just for me. He left an indelible impression on me that is still impacting my life. He listened to me like a father when no one else did, he counseled me as a father figure, and he encouraged me. In fact, knowing my situation at home, I think he extended me special attention. Furthermore, he showed me that there was a way to live differently from the examples of the other men in my life.

He showed me how to treat women by the way he treated Marty, his wife. He showed me what a godly marriage and a Christian home looked like. I can't remember how many hours I spent in his home with him and his delightful wife and children.

Then, in my twenties, I had the privilege of ministering under a pastor who furthered and continued my life education. Milan Yerkovich modeled what a Christian husband ought to be so wonderfully and genuinely and—this is important—so close to me that I couldn't miss it. For two years he met with me and another man every week to pray together, talk together, and grow spiritually together. Milan was, like Gene Lacy before, God's provision for me.

When the replacements work better than the original

I had no earthly father qualified to show me what I needed to be a good husband and father. And it would have taken, as we often say too glibly, "a miracle" for me to overcome these handicaps.

But God not only helped me to overcome them, He provided these examples so that He could in turn use me to teach other men how to be godly fathers and husbands. I bear the loving brand of Gene and Marty Lacy and Milan and Kay Yerkovich on my life. They were the miracles, not me. They not only affected me, they have also influenced my wife and children. God used them to break a family legacy that was heading downward at a rapid rate.

Many times I have shaken my head in silent amazement as God has used me to counsel troubled couples, or speak to others about raising children, or to write articles about being a husband or father. Many of those I help had far better role models in their natural fathers than I.

I also cannot tell you how many times my eyes have filled with tears in gratitude as I thank God for my wonderful relationship with my wife, Annette, and my children.

Miracles? None. But you would never be able to convince me God was not supernaturally behind these events. These two godly men were probably praying one day to have an impact on someone's life for Christ, and then I showed up with all my weaknesses and problems. Coincidence? Not in my book. My heavenly Father saw to it that I was given what I consider to be the best this world has to offer in male Christian role models.

The unexpected miracles

When my earthly male parental role model failed, and hurt me deeply, I admit that I wondered what God was doing. I had prayed for help, expecting *a certain kind of miracle*. God didn't send the kind of miracle I expected; He sent a far, far better one. It wasn't the blatant kind of miracle we usually ask for, it was much more like the Esther variety—hidden, behind the scenes, viewed most clearly in retrospect.

Have you been wondering where God is lately? Have you entered a crisis and prayed, and yet it seems God doesn't answer you. Does it seem as if He's abandoned you, as if He isn't interested in your life anymore? Have you been trying to make sense of His silence? Have you been asking God for *a certain kind of miracle?*

The book of Esther assures us that He is *totally* aware of our situation and *actively* working in ways that we couldn't begin to imagine. Remember, God occasionally chooses to use miracles, but He never needs to.

Living in fear, learning through faith

The first time I took my oldest daughter, Christi, on the Matterhorn roller coaster at Disneyland, she looked terrified during the first part of the ride. You see, she had no way of knowing, at five years of age, whether the roller coaster would crash, as it occasionally seems it will, or whether it would turn just in time to avoid the next rock.

Noticing her frightened look, I managed to get her attention and began shouting and laughing, "Isn't this fun?"

In just a matter of seconds she too was laughing and giggling.

She wasn't sure about the ride at first, but her confidence in me and the fact that she knew I wouldn't let anything happen to her allowed her to relax and enjoy herself. In the same way God often uses crisis points, scary rides in our lives, to cause us to learn to trust in Him and His providential care for us.

As we close this chapter, I urge you to stop here for a moment and take any area of concern or crisis in your life and give it to God in prayer. Be honest with God. Go ahead and say, "I've been real worried about this, Lord, afraid You weren't with me, afraid I was on my own, unsure of Your presence in this situation. Help me to realize that You are active even when I can't see You or feel You. Give me the assurance of Your providential care in this great issue of my life. Help me to begin to see Your shadow."

I know how it can appear at times as if God is much like an overworked divine social worker: well-intentioned, but unable to adequately keep track of your situation. It seems that by the time He gets around to your crisis the damage has already been done. If we were honest, we'd admit that we felt He truly wasn't paying attention, that He was somehow distracted.

We will soon see, however, that far from being distracted, God has been backstage, working diligently on your case, years before your first inkling that there would ever be a crisis.

Two

Backstage Choreography

Profiles from the book of Esther

When I was a young boy my family used to visit the Dorothy Chandler Pavilion in Los Angeles and enjoy the latest and best stage productions. Before each performance would begin (which seemed an interminably long time for a young boy), I would leaf through the program to find the short biographies of each actor in the play. While short, they provided tantalizing insight into the real-life backgrounds of the actors, their past roles, and interesting tidbits about their personal lives.

This little bit of background prepared me to fully appreciate and enjoy the history of each person prior to his or her involvement in this production. It also helped me to see the actors as people before I saw them in their roles.

They came from diverse backgrounds and experiences. Some came from the Shakespearean stage, others from TV appearances or singing careers, and yet they were all brought together by the director to star in this production.

The book of Esther has been properly dubbed by various commentators as a drama. It is an elaborate production divinely staged and designed to enlighten the audience to the ever-present, though invisible, care of a loving God in the midst of crisis. However, before the real-life drama begins, we will see that God has been busily orchestrating the events of the lives of all the main characters in preparation for this moment of crisis.

Circumstances in the lives of different people, seemingly unconnected to each other, would in the end finish the puzzle of God's perfect will. At the same time we are going to see that each of the main characters is a unique story.

As the curtain opens on the book of Esther the first character to appear is the royal and mighty:

King Ahasuerus: The Powerful Pawn of God

Ahasuerus (pronounced a-haz-u-é-rus) was the king's Persian name, but we know him in history as Xerxes, who reigned from 485–465 B.C. He was famous for launching one of the greatest armies ever assembled, to conquer Greece.

In the first chapter of Esther, Ahasuerus gives a royal banquet for his princes and VIPs. Persians were famous for their elaborate banquets and lavish parties which could last months. Some historians believe that this party Ahasuerus gave was designed to enlist the support of his officers for his upcoming campaign against Greece.

He wanted to convince them he had the resources to fund this great venture, and what better way than to show off his wealth? Could a man with these resources possibly be defeated?

For one hundred eighty days he wined and dined them, arranging hunts in the royal parks, horse races, chariot races, and mock battles. But the ostentatious coup-de-gras came when they were allowed to view carefully selected objects from the royal treasury. This was an empire exhibition, a sort of World's Fair or Expo 482 B.C.

There were alabaster and marble dishes, and even one whole wall given over to personal jewelry, hair ornaments, bracelets inlaid with garnet, amethyst, turquoise, and lapis, and necklaces with thick gold lace. Lying loose in dishes like finger candy were pearls and emeralds by the handsful, turquoise, and lapis lazuli. Everywhere they looked gold was in abundance.

The color scheme would dazzle the eyes—green, white, blue, with cords of fine linen fastened to silver rings attached to marble pillars. Beds were of gold and silver against a backdrop of red, white, blue, and black marble.

Danger: volatile mixture

Yet history relates some events in the life of Ahasuerus that shed light on his temperament and help us to get an idea of the volatile nature of the man. For example, in his military campaign against Greece, he once ordered a bridge to be built over the Hellespont, a channel of water between the Sea of Marmara and the Aegean Sea that separates Greece and Turkey.

However, upon completion of the great project, and just before he was able to use it, a storm came and completely destroyed the bridge. This so infuriated him that he ordered his officers to give the sea three hundred lashes as punishment, and he had a pair of leg irons thrown into the sea at the point where the bridge had collapsed, as if he had the authority to punish the elements themselves. Then, he had all the builders of the bridge beheaded. Such was his temper and his rash abuse of power.

On the same campaign he was offered a fortune by a loyal citizen named Pythius, a Lydian, toward the expenses of his military expedition. All of Pythius's five sons were serving in the army of Ahasuerus. Overjoyed at Pythius's loyalty, he returned the money, giving Pythius a generous gift besides.

But shortly after, when this same Pythius humbly requested that one of his five sons might remain at home to look after him in his declining years, an enraged Ahasuerus had Pythius's son cut in two and ordered his armies to march between the severed halves of his body.

Herodotus, the ancient historian, tells us that among the thousands of leaders gathered for the Persian expedition against Greece, Ahasuerus was the most attractive, most regal, and most dignified. He had a stately and royal bearing, but emotionally and morally he was a mixture of passionate and unpredictable extremes.

After the humiliation of his military defeat at the hands of Greece he drowned his sorrows in such a plunge of sensuality that he publicly offered a prize for the invention of some new physical indulgence to relieve his misery.

His vast resources, gigantic notions, and notorious temper made him the awe of the ancient world. And yet this same Ahasuerus, to whom his subjects bowed as the very image of God, an absolute tyrannical monarch, is shown to be simply the powerful pawn of God.

It is natural to look at powerful people from a strictly human perspective and quake with fear. These people are in control of our lives. We have a feeling of helplessness being under tyrannical bosses, or dictatorial leaders, or domineering spouses, or unreasonable parents. We can believe there is no hope, that nothing can be done because they're in control. What God demonstrates through Ahasuerus is that He alone is in control.

As Christians we need to rediscover the power behind the powers that be. Your fate is not in your boss's hands, or your political leader's hands, or your spouse's hands, or your parent's hands, or the voter's hands, or the congregation's hands—it is in God's hands.

The Ahasueruses of our lives have their purposes and God uses them, but they have no control over the outcome of our lives. The future is firmly in God's hands. We see here that God was in the shadows, backstage, choreographing Ahasuerus's part in His great deliverance.

But, the scene soon shifts from the king to his wife:

Queen Vashti: The Woman with a Loose Grip on Security

Vashti is one of the most tragic of all the characters in the book of Esther. Not very much is told about Vashti, except that she was Ahasuerus's wife, and that she was very beautiful. It is likely that she was one of the most beautiful women in the kingdom.

We know that she must also have been intelligent and cultured. Her royal duties were extensive. At the same time the king was giving his royal banquet for his officers and VIPs, she was hosting a royal banquet for their wives. She couldn't have been a brainless beauty.

We know from history that Persian kings had several harems containing hundreds of beautiful women chosen from the great Persian Empire after extensive beauty hunts, so Queen Vashti was surely the cream of the crop. The king was obviously proud of her, so proud that he wanted to show her off before his drunken officers and leaders. When she refused to come, her fate was sealed.

Perched on the edge of a cliff

Vashti had everything going for her: money, position, security, power, and looks. She was at the top looking down, but she was perched precariously close to the edge of the cliff. Out of hundreds of beautiful women in the several large harems of the king she alone had been chosen to be his queen. But her life contained one tragic flaw: all she had was attached to Ahasuerus! Her entire security in life was connected to a man, the king. And in a moment, through really no fault of her own, she lost it all. The king deposed her over one act.

God had given her many privileges and gifts other women didn't possess. Almost any woman in the kingdom would have traded places with her. She was the First Lady. But while God gave her many wonderful privileges, they were only temporary.

While it is unlikely Vashti was killed, she would never again enjoy the elite and privileged position she had come to enjoy, and she must have languished in disgrace, permanently alienated from all that had defined her success. Her descent from fame to shame happened overnight. She must have become the tragic object of rumor and speculation.

Later we will see that Esther was willing to voluntarily give up the same position because of her faith. Her position, her power, and affluence did not own her. She wasn't forced to give it up, she volunteered to lose not only her position, but her very life. Esther's faith provided a greater security than the great Persian Empire could. The pagan religion that the Persians, and assuredly Vashti, clung to, could not.

Skating on thin ice

If our security or sense of identity rests in someone or something that can be taken away from us, we're skating through life on thin ice, because we don't know where the cracks are hidden. We're not guaranteed that we won't lose that person we are leaning on or that job, or fame, or status, or lifestyle that we are depending on to give us our identity.

C. S. Lewis, in a chapter titled "The Business of Heaven," emphasizes the danger of pinning your faith on people. He writes:

Do not forget this. At first it is natural for a baby to take its mother's milk without knowing its mother. It is equally natural for us to see the man who helps us without seeing Christ behind him. But we must not remain babies. We must go on to recognize the real Giver. It is madness not to. Because, if we do not, we shall be relying on human beings. And that is going to let us down. The best of them will make mistakes; all of them will die. We must be thankful to all the people who have helped us, we must honour and love them. But never, never pin your whole faith on any human being: not if he is the best and wisest in the whole world. There are lots of nice things you can do with sand; but do not try building a house on it.[1]

Vashti's house was built on sand. Her position and privileges were only temporary.

Several years ago I received a letter from the superintendent of our denomination. We had been praying for his wife, who was diagnosed with terminal cancer. Even though the most important person in his life was terminally ill and God was apparently choosing not to heal her, his faith in God was never shaken, nor was his wife's faith deterred. He wrote:

First, let me thank all of you for the wonderful sense of your support and prayers that we have experienced. God has given both Gail [not her real name] and me a real sense of His peace through these days. Gail has been absolutely a champ through it all. She trusts the Lord so completely that it is an encouragement to all who visit her. At the present time she is doing remarkably well for someone with cancer in her liver. She gets up and dresses herself and does whatever she can for herself. Please continue to pray in these ways. First, that the low grade fever that she has most of the time will be removed. She breaks into a heavy sweat and it breaks for a short time, but it always returns. Secondly, our united prayer is that if God can be glorified by it, He will choose to heal her.

At the bottom of the letter he wrote a simple sentence that exposed the tight grip he has on God, his security. "Finally, I believe what I have preached about our Lord for over 40 years more passionately than ever."

----

1. C. S. Lewis, "The Business of Heaven," *The Inspirational Writings of C.S. Lewis.* New York: Inspirational Press, 1987, 494.

Checking your anchor

Have you checked what the anchor of your life is resting on lately? A seminary professor of mine once shared that "if your security in life is dependent upon someone who can be taken away from you, or something you can lose, you're living a precarious existence."

Vashti, the woman with a loose grip on security, fades into the background. God removed the person she was leaning on, and what she sought so fervently to prevent in front of Ahasuerus's drunken cronies ironically occurs. She is spiritually exposed as being truly naked in the crisis of her life. However, as she fades into the background, a new character emerges on the scene.

Mordecai: Faithful the Second Time Around

Being one of the heroes of the book, this may seem a strange label, but we know that Mordecai did not heed the call of the prophets Isaiah and Jeremiah, who were speaking on behalf of God. These prophets had called upon the Jews in exile to *leave* their captivity. Cyrus, the great Persian ruler, who had overthrown the Babylonian Empire, had earlier given the Jews permission to go back and rebuild their temple and reinstitute the temple offerings and worship.

Cyrus had called upon every Jew in his empire to return to Jerusalem, the Holy City, to their own lands, with his blessing. This was in fulfillment of prophecy (Isaiah 44:28).

Thus says Cyrus king of Persia, "The LORD, the God of heaven, has given me all the kingdoms of the earth, and He has appointed me to build Him a house in Jerusalem, which is in Judah. Whoever there is among you of all His people, may his God be with him! Let him go up to Jerusalem which is in Judah, and rebuild the house of the LORD, the God of Israel; He is the God who is in Jerusalem." (Ezra 1:2–3)

Isaiah 48:20 and Jeremiah 50:8 and 51:6, 9 confirm this.

Misplaced priorities

Though Persia had overthrown the Babylonian Empire at this time, Babylon still existed, and the command was firm, they were to leave their place of captivity. Mordecai didn't listen. We don't know the reasons or the excuses. They may have seemed wise at the time, but the command of God was clear. He should have left. Maybe it was the good job he had in the government, or family ties in Persia; we don't know. What we do know is that returning to rebuild the temple of God should have been his priority.

God's response to Mordecai was gracious, however. The truth is that those several million Jews living in Persia, who had ignored God's clear direction, had not been ignored by God in spite of their disobedience.

Despite our unfaithfulness God still watches over us. We've all made mistakes that we wish we hadn't made, spoken words we wish we could take back, done things we wish we hadn't done. They're done—history—but we often let those mistakes handicap our future service.

We can easily begin to think, "I've made so many bad choices with my life it's too late to do anything worthwhile." Or, "I've messed up my life so bad God can never use me now." It's easy to believe that God must be as disgusted with all our failures as we are, so He's probably thrown in the towel on us.

The lesson of Mordecai is that God's faithfulness to us is not dependent upon our faithfulness to Him. And our unfaithfulness to Him never leads to His unfaithfulness to us.

Mistakes, failures, and other fertilizers

God still desires to use our lives to accomplish great things for His kingdom. God doesn't remove us from the game of life when we make mistakes. In fact, He's willing to take those mistakes and failures of ours and design something beautiful from them, if we'll let Him.

It is not uncommon in the Sierras to see a dead, fallen tree, slowly turning to mulch, a victim of fire, disease, or lightning. Yet out of that death and decay grows a new tree, bright, green, and healthy. The dead tree provides the nourishment and bed for new growth.

Mordecai exhibits reverence for God and obedience in some tough situations in the account of Esther. He *did* have faith in God, he *did* pray and fast before God, and he *didn't* let the past dictate his future.

Mordecai put his faith on the back burner once by not going back to his homeland, but he doesn't do it this time. God didn't bench Mordecai because of past mistakes or shortcomings. Behind the scenes, God redirected Mordecai's life so that he eventually becomes part of the Jews' great deliverance.

At any point in our lives, in spite of past shortcomings, mistakes, and failures, the promise of God stands: "Those who honor Me I will honor" (1 Samuel 2:30).

In His time, and in His way. As Chuck Swindoll so often wisely reminds us, "It's never too late to start doing what is right . . . never!"

As Mordecai is ushered off stage, a new character, our main character, is ushered on.

Esther: Person of Privilege, Person of Responsibility

It is through the example of Esther that we learn one of the greatest lessons of the book, that God gives us blessings and gifts *in trust!* He makes us stewards or caretakers of them, but often requires us to be willing to unconditionally relinquish them to accomplish His purposes.

Esther was an orphan Jewess, given over to the care of her older cousin Mordecai. God had given Esther several gifts, including her great beauty and Mordecai for a relative. When Vashti was deposed, Esther ascended to the position of queen, through an empire-wide hunt. She was then given incredible privilege and lavish wealth. Esther came by all of these blessings providentially.

God had been in the shadows of Esther's life, orchestrating situations that would prove beneficial to His plans for her. But Esther also proves a good steward of what she was given. She did not cling jealously to the blessings she received, but when God requested that she relinquish her claim on them, she was willing to give them up.

God gives us our positions for His purposes, not simply our own enjoyment. And He requires that we be willing to relinquish them in order to accomplish His perfect will. He doesn't always *require* that we relinquish them, but He asks us to be *willing* to.

Taking bows for God's performances

Esther was a person of privilege and a person of responsibility. So are we. Too often we lose perspective on what occurs in our lives. We are given money to buy our first house, or we happen to be in the right place at the right time for a promotion, or we inherit money, or we are born with beauty, great talent, or ability—things that are, in reality, completely out of our control. God providentially gives them to us. As Paul once reminded the Corinthian church: "What do you have that you did not receive? But if you did receive it, why do you boast as if you had not received it?" (1 Corinthians 4:7).

We rejoice in the blessings, but fail often to recognize the responsibility. Exploiting the blessings to our own advantage, we can ignore the responsibilities that inherently go along with them. In fact, if we're not careful, we can begin to believe that we were the cause of everything that has happened to us and begin to take credit for things we had no control over. We can start taking bows for God's work.

In Esther we will see a wonderful example of a person of privilege and a person of responsibility—a person of physical beauty and high social standing who uses those blessings for the preservation of those less fortunate.

Finally, there is one last character to appear in the book of Esther. The star of the tragedy:

Haman: The Man Who Hung Himself

Haman enters in chapter 3 and appears as the rising star in the kingdom. His success was meteoric. He was on the high road and fast track to success, and nothing was going to stop him. He was overconfident, arrogant, conceited, abusively powerful, and uncontentedly rich. *People* magazine would have loved this guy!

He had been given tremendous honor and power, and yet we see in the account of Esther that he always wanted more. He wouldn't let anything get between him and his pursuit of more. He literally became a victim of his own invention.

He had been chosen by Ahasuerus as prime minister of the great Persian Empire, and greater glory surely would have followed, except that he couldn't see that his actions in seeking to destroy Mordecai and all the Jews were placing him in opposition to the God of heaven. When Mordecai refused to bow before him, it seemed a small thing to Haman to dispose of several million inconsequential Jews. Here was a man with a Final Solution thousands of years before Hitler.

A victim of his own appetite

He had everything but contentment, and his lust for more power devoured him in the end. He died with the most toys, but he didn't win. The gallows he had built for Mordecai the Jew, the one person who wouldn't bow down to him, was the gallows he swung from himself.

The Eskimos, I am told, have a cunning way of killing wolves. Instead of going out and hunting them, they have devised an ingenious method of destruction. They search out areas where wolves traffic and plant a knife in the snow, with the handle hidden, and just the blade sticking up. Then they cover the blade with blood and bits of raw flesh, allowing it to freeze and become hard.

The wolves, with their highly developed sense of smell, quickly come upon the frozen blood. Sensing a dead animal, they begin to lick at the blood. The more they lick, the warmer the blood becomes, and the wolves work up to a frenzy, driven by their lust for blood. They lick more and more aggressively until they begin to cut their tongues on the blade, but they don't realize it because their own warm blood begins to flow and further feeds the frenzy. They slowly bleed to death, victims of their own appetite.

Haman determined his own fate when he foolishly laid claim to the lives of God's people. Spurning the power of the God of heaven, lulled into overconfidence by God's silence, he determined his own end.

And what's the final picture of Haman, the self-made millionaire, power player, and egotist? It's pathetic. He's crying and begging mercy at the feet of a Jewish woman! You've got to appreciate the irony of it! No man can touch him, but God brings him down with an orphan Jewish girl.

These are the main characters of the book of Esther, each one a story, and yet all together they are grand examples of God working providentially in the shadows to accomplish His will and to provide protection for His people.

Ahasuerus: The powerful pawn of God.
Vashti: The woman with a loose grip on security.
Mordecai: Faithful the second time around.
Esther: Person of privilege, person of responsibility.
Haman: The man who hung himself.

Backstage choreography! God is in control and busily orchestrating the events of our lives to draw us closer to Himself and to accomplish His purposes in our lives. The purpose of the book of Esther is to open our eyes to see God in a way we never have before—not as a silent, absent God, but as a vitally active, involved, and interested God.

But, while God does orchestrate events in our lives, we are by no means robots, victims of divine fate. On the contrary. We will soon see how God directs our lives through decisions we have made, even decisions we made long ago.

Three

Setting the Stage

I can still remember the picture vividly in my mind. I was sitting in front of my television set watching the evening news when a tragic story came on. As the story was narrated by a newscaster, a homemade video, taken by a local bystander, showed the gripping spectacle of an aging trapeze artist in Europe trying to get some publicity. He was walking a tightrope at a great height between two buildings. The tightrope walker had done this all his life for a circus; he was vastly experienced.

Calmly and confidently, almost nonchalantly, he went about his feat. I was in more danger of being hit by a bus in my living room than he was of falling off of that familiar line he had walked so many times before. To give the crowd some extra "Wow!" he was performing without a net. He had done this thousands of times before. Then . . . he fell.

It was that quick, that simple, and that horrible. He never cried out, he simply fell to his death.

When you think about it, this man's fate had been determined the moment he chose to make a living out of defying the law of gravity. His job involved gambling—big time! The law of gravity is certain and unchangeable; his level of skill and the conditions were the only variables. Unknown to many of us, principles we have chosen to live by, decisions made many years earlier, perhaps even in our youth, will have a tremendous effect on our lives. They have set the stage for our lives.

In the grand scheme of creation, God spoke truths designed to help us maneuver through the jagged rocks and whitewater rapids of life. Those truths are like the law of gravity, certain and unchangeable. Behind the scenes God is silently ordering our lives according to our response to His truths.

We're going to see in Esther that the stage was set for certain events long before the crisis ever occurred, because of the life principles our main characters had chosen.

Each principle becomes evident as we observe their lives and the direction they took. Because of their choices the outcome was never in doubt. God often uses our responses to His principles and truths to set the stage for the events of our lives.

Ahasuerus

In the first ten verses of the book of Esther we get a little of the history of Ahasuerus. Here we are told of a magnificent display of wealth and power. The ostentatious display had a purpose: to prove to everyone that he had all the resources necessary to launch a costly and difficult campaign. He wanted to make it clear that the end result was not in doubt, he *was* going to win.

Ahasuerus's destiny was set in motion the moment he bought into the lie that our fate, our destiny, is in our own hands. If we just plan well, work hard, and don't quit we will ultimately *have* to taste the success we're reaching for.

It's a simple formula: human ingenuity + hard work = the realization of our dreams. Sound familiar? It's also the American creed. Ahasuerus had mapped out his life and what should happen, but he left God out of the picture, and in so doing he set himself up for a fall.

We know from history that Ahasuerus did amass a great army and set out to conquer Greece, but was defeated. This battle should have been a blowout of major proportions. This was the Dallas Cowboys against the local high school team. With all the resources available to Ahasuerus, he couldn't lose. All the conventional wisdom was on the side of the Persians. But he lost!

Like father like son

Greece was always a burr under his royal saddle. When Ahasuerus's father sent messengers to the Athenians for the tokens of submission, earth and water, his messengers were unceremoniously thrown into a well and told to find their tokens there. The messengers sent to Sparta never returned.

He came from a long line of conquering kings. His pride could not permit such affronts to his royal person. And remember, he had resources to fight a long and protracted war.

His pride must have burst the royal seams as his enormous and exotic army passed before him on parade. The army was so large it took days to complete the review of his troops. They came from every country in Asia, along with Egypt and Ethiopia; it even included Jews. In addition to his great army, he had a fleet of hundreds of ships, but this great fleet was defeated by the Greeks at the famous battle of Salamis.

After the final defeat at Salamis he withdrew from the campaign, and a year later it was discontinued. During the remainder of his reign, Ahasuerus seems to have given up all interest in reigning. He spent a boring existence absorbed in, if you can believe it, the intrigues of his harem. He left the governing to his ministers and cronies (often slaves), and he was finally murdered by one of his high-ranking officials.

The stage was set for his end when he bought into the belief that

Success in Life Is All in the Planning

Up to that point in his life it had probably worked. If we plan for success and then achieve it, we get sore arms from patting ourselves on the back for our ingenuity.

We see it only as a successful formula, nothing else. It's conventional wisdom, accepted everywhere. But it crashes into the truths found in God's Word.

Listen to the words of the psalms:

> The LORD nullifies the counsel of the nations;
> He frustrates the plans of the peoples.
> The counsel of the LORD stands forever,

The plans of His heart from generation to generation. . . .
The king is not saved by a mighty army;
A warrior is not delivered by great strength.
A horse is a false hope for victory;
Nor does it deliver anyone by its great strength.

(Psalm 33:10–11, 16–17)

Ahasuerus's fragile life crashed against the rock-hard principles of God's words and was shattered and broken, scattered upon the dust heap of history. We are encouraged to think and plan ahead, but if we don't acknowledge God in the outcome, we are setting ourselves up for a fall.

Proverbs 16:1 says, "The plans of the heart belong to man [go ahead and plan], *but* the answer of the tongue is from the LORD" (italics mine).

The outcome is not in our hands, but in His. Thus, as Proverbs 16:3 says, "Commit your works to the LORD, and your plans will be established."

Success in life is not all in the planning; it is in the acknowledging of God in every aspect of our lives, and releasing the outcome to His will. The stage was set for Ahasuerus's life the moment he bought into the lie that success in life is all in the planning.

Mordecai

We find that the stage had also been set earlier in Mordecai's life for the events that would unfold.

I am reminded of an accountant I once knew who had recently become a Christian. A few months after he became a Christian his company asked him to alter their books, to lie about financial statements.

All of a sudden his obedience to God was challenged. He didn't know what would happen if he refused, although I'm sure he guessed, but He had given his life to Christ, and wanted to be obedient, so he refused. Under false pretenses, his boss fired him!

Pledging allegiance and obedience to God when nothing is at stake can be inspirational and exciting, but facing a very real cost for that same obedience and allegiance is quite another thing.

I'm sure that the accountant must have been wondering about the cost of his obedience at this point. He had been making a lot of money and had a lot of nice things, but like many others, didn't have much in the bank. He wasn't planning for a catastrophe, few of us do. He lost everything, and he and his family lived for many months dependent upon the kindness of other Christians until he could get on his feet again.

Eventually he got a new job and was able to see God's provision in it. But his obedience cost him; it didn't come cheaply.

In chapter 3 we find Mordecai refusing to bow down to Haman, Ahasuerus's hand-picked prime minister. The honor the Persians paid Haman upon his promotion was akin to that of the honor they paid Ahasuerus, whom they considered to be like God. All of a sudden Mordecai's faith had a price tag. He was not allowed to worship any man, only God (Esther 3:2–4).

The cost? His life and the life of every Jew in the empire, decreed by the king under the manipulation of Haman.

That's the problem with obedience: at first it seems that the price is too high. God *can't* expect me to pay this high a price. He must want me to give in on this one issue, there is simply too much at stake.

There are times when we are obedient as was each of these men and the initial result is calamity. Then we become confused. We say to ourselves, "I thought God blessed obedience, and look, I was obedient and the situation got *worse!*" God does promise blessings for obedience, but He does not promise them in the way we expect them, or in the time we expect them.

For Mordecai, the principle guiding his life was:

The Price of Obedience Is Never Too High

The truth is that we encounter many situations in life that seem to challenge this principle. We know that obedience to God is a must for those who call Christ *Lord.* Jesus said in John 14:15, "If you love Me you will keep My commandments." This was nothing new. The problem is that obedience often comes sporting an expensive price tag.

In contrast to his earlier failure to heed the call of God to return to Jerusalem, Mordecai determines to live by obedience now regardless of the cost, showing that we can change the direction our lives are headed.

The stage was set for Mordecai's life the moment he bought into the principle that the price of obedience is never too high. When we sense the silence of God we are apt to overlook this principle in favor of something with swifter and more beneficial results. When our obedience to God causes things to get quickly worse (we get fired, lose a promotion, get ridiculed for taking a moral stand, or lose the man or woman of our dreams) and we call out to God and He doesn't instantly change things for the better, we can be sorely tempted to forego obedience for something less costly.

The example of Mordecai shows again that even when God doesn't immediately act in a way we'd hoped, His commitment to blessing obedience is assured.

But following on the heels of Mordecai in chapter two is Esther, our main character.

Esther

In the second chapter (2:8–18) we follow the account of Esther becoming queen. From her being selected to be a possible candidate for queen, to her quickly gaining favor with the king's beauty and talent scouts. She was given seven beauty attendants from the palace and transferred to the best place in the harem. She could see her star rising. But while she was receiving all this attention, she continued to listen to Mordecai.

She continued her relationship with Mordecai because they were related not just by blood, but by faith. She could have easily abandoned her relationship with him when she became queen, but she didn't! In fact, because she still continued her relationship with him, which represented her ties to her Jewish religion and her faith in God, Ahasuerus was saved from an assassination plot uncovered by Mordecai.

Here we find the presence of the principle that was to guide her life and her actions in the events to come. We find Esther clinging to the principle that:

What I Am Is More Important Than What I Have

Her security, her sense of identity, was not tied up in Ahasuerus like Vashti's had been, it was tied up in God. She was Esther the child of God, first; Esther, the queen of the Persian Empire, second. That gave her life the equilibrium and perspective that is so often missing these days.

How often have we seen young athletes out of high school and college go from poor, underprivileged neighborhoods into lifestyles where they are making millions, but their lives begin to unravel. Many of them become hooked on drugs and the trappings of the fast lane because their only identity is their new lifestyle, and they have no way to keep it all in perspective.

People inherit millions of dollars, or win a lottery, and yet when you go back and look at the results years later, you usually find tragedy! Their new fortunes have actually hurt them rather than helped them.

Esther was a child of God, and that identity was more important than any title or position she could receive. Keeping her relationship with Mordecai, which was her tie to her faith in God, was the very thing that saved her life and the lives of all the Jews in Persia.

But don't you see? The stage was set for her deliverance the moment she bought into the principle that what I am is more important than what I have.

Finally, there is one last character whose life and direction was set in motion by the principle for living that he clung to.

Haman

In the beginning of chapter 3 of the book of Esther, Haman is promoted to the number two position in the empire.

The people were commanded by the king to treat him as they would the king himself, bowing down in reverence as to a god. But Mordecai refuses and it infuriates Haman.

> When Haman saw that Mordecai neither bowed down nor paid homage to him, Haman was filled with rage. But he disdained to lay hands on Mordecai alone, for they had told him who the people of Mordecai were; therefore Haman sought to destroy all the Jews, the people of Mordecai, who were throughout the whole kingdom of Ahasuerus. (Esther 3:5–6)

Now the Hebrews weren't the only ones who wouldn't bow down to men. The Greeks did not believe in bowing down to men either, and I'm sure that Haman likely dealt with Greeks in his position in the government. But instead of letting this incident pass, he made revenge his quest. All his conquests to date weren't enough, he needed just one more!

He was at the top of the heap, and he could have just enjoyed what he had achieved, ignoring this low-level bureaucrat and his insignificant religion. But he couldn't.

Let's look ahead a few chapters:

> Then Haman recounted to them the glory of his riches, and the number of his sons, and every instance where the king had magnified him, and how he had promoted him above the princes and servants of the king. Haman also said, "Even Esther the queen let no one but me come with the king to the banquet which she had prepared; and tomorrow also I am invited by her with the king. Yet all of this does not satisfy me every time I see Mordecai the Jew sitting at the king's gate." (Esther 5:11–13)

"Yet all of this does not satisfy me." Other than royalty, no one in Haman's world held greater power and prestige than he. He had reached the pinnacle of success. Yet, there is nothing new in this attitude, it's as old as human nature. Solomon said in the Proverbs: "Sheol and Abaddon are never satisfied, nor are the eyes of man ever satisfied" (Proverbs 27:20).

The principle for living that best sums up Haman's life is:

You Can Never Have Too Much

While this hits a little too close to home to be comfortable, the truth is that Haman was just like you and me, except that he had access to the things we can only dream of. It's an affliction of our sinful nature. Solomon wrote some other timeless words in Ecclesiastes which hit home.

There is an evil which I have seen under the sun and it is prevalent among men—a man to whom God has given riches and wealth and honor so that his soul lacks nothing of all that he desires, but God has not empowered him to eat from them, for a foreigner enjoys them. This is vanity and a severe affliction. If a man fathers a hundred children and lives many years, however many they be, but his soul is not satisfied with good things, and he does not even have a proper burial, then I say, "Better the miscarriage than he, for it comes in futility and goes into obscurity; and its name is covered in obscurity." (Ecclesiastes 6:1–4)

Someone once defined *failure* as "living without knowing what life is all about, feeding on things that do not satisfy, thinking you have everything, only to find out in the end you have nothing that matters." History confirms these truths over and over again.

Success—twenty-five years later

In 1923 there was a gathering in Chicago of the world's most successful financiers of that day. Newspapers and magazines printed their success stories, and urged American youth to follow their examples. Collectively these tycoons controlled more wealth than there was in the U.S. Treasury. But someone followed their lives and reported on what had become of them twenty-five years later.

Charles Schwab, president of the largest steel company—lived on borrowed money the last five years of his life. He died broke.

Arthur Cutten, the greatest wheat speculator—died abroad, insolvent.

Richard Whitney, president of the New York Stock Exchange—twenty-five years later was being released from prison.

Albert Fali, a member of the president's cabinet—was pardoned from prison so he could die at home.

Jessee Livermore, the greatest "bear" on Wall Street—committed suicide.

Leon Fraser, president of the Bank of International Settlements—committed suicide.

Ivar Grueger, head of the world's largest monopoly—committed suicide.

What will history eventually tell us about today's heroes? Money wasn't the issue for any of these men, contentment was. Many people buy into the lie that you have to have a little more to be satisfied. What they have isn't enough. The funny thing is, it has nothing to do with money, or what you have or don't have.

The stuff isn't the issue, our attitude toward it is. There is nothing wrong with trying to get ahead, or with making a better life for yourself, but if you aren't happy with what you have now, you won't be happy with more either, because there will *always* be something you don't or can't have. Make sense?

Think about it. Has a little more ever provided that *permanent* contentment for you? If you're honest, you'll admit it hasn't. We can never be content until we can honestly say, "I have enough," and mean it.

The stage was set for Haman's life the moment he bought fully into the principle for living that you can never have enough. He lived life hungry, never satisfied, never content.

Four principles for living: two in direct violation of the truths of God's Word, and Ahasuerus and Haman crashed their lives on the truths of God's words; two in direct compliance with the truths of God's words, and Esther and Mordecai found protection under the shelter of God's truth.

For those of you who *have* been faithful, whose integrity and obedience have seen a high price tag and yet you have faithfully paid it, don't quit, don't be discouraged. The apostle Paul says, "Let us not lose heart in doing good, for in due time we shall reap if we do not grow weary" (Galatians 6:9).

Don't give up, it *is* all worth it. God *is* on the throne, He *does* see, and He *will* reward . . . in His time—because God *is* in control.

Behind the scenes God is silently choreographing our lives according to our response to His truths. Though we do not see Him, His movements and activity are predictable.

But while God does bless our obedience to His Word in many ways, there is not always an immediate reward, as we will see. In fact, there are times when the things God will request of us will seem downright unreasonable—almost self-destructive, as Esther was soon to discover.

Four

Difficult Parts to Play

I've got a confession to make. I'm a dyed-in-the-wool, 24-carat, authentic rut person. I like ruts. No, I *love* ruts! Ruts are predictable, safe, familiar, and easy to maneuver in (because you don't have to make any sudden changes). Routine brings me a sense of peace and well-being.

I like knowing what to expect. I like things to turn out exactly the way they are supposed to. My wife agrees that I have a romance with ruts. The problem is that as a Christian I sometimes find them a little hard to come by.

The reason I like ruts so much is that they can insulate me from the pain and stress of change, from ever changing my habits, thoughts, language, perceptions, or values; and change is precisely what God has in mind for me. So He often upsets my routine, moving me away from the familiar into uncharted territory.

Have you ever noticed that there are times in our lives when God directs us into situations that are unfamiliar, re-

quiring us to play difficult parts? They roughly jar us out
of our comfortable smooth ruts and put us again on
bumpy, rough roads. We feel unprepared, inadequate,
overwhelmed, outnumbered, and frightened.

Walking the plank

God has never asked this kind of thing from us before,
and we feel we're not ready, or the time isn't right, or too
many things are up in the air, and we want to back out of
the situation, and yet, we can't. We're stuck! We can't go
back to our comfortable ruts, and yet we feel that walking
forward is tantamount to walking the plank! It seems like a
no-win situation! We can't believe God is asking this of us,
or that He would put us in this situation. When we question
what He's doing we are met with a predictable, but frustrating, silence.

What we don't know is that God has been preparing us
all our lives for these very moments. We're more prepared
than we imagine. Every movement of God in the past has
been in preparation for this day, this hour, this very moment.

We will see that we aren't the first. Esther before us was
similarly asked to play just such a difficult part, and she
heard no more from God than we do. Yet, in spite of God's
silence, Esther found she was prepared.

We're going to see that the steps that God asked Esther
to take are the very same steps that He often asks us to take.
God is going to ask Esther to

Walk by Faith into the Jaws of Negative Circumstances

When Haman brazenly asked the king to make a decree
that the Jews be destroyed, the king, uninterested in such

mundane issues of governing, rubber-stamped Haman's request, and the horrible deed was set into motion.

Mordecai, horrified at the news, eventually contacted Esther, and unapologetically called on her to intervene.

In verse 8 we find the crucial statement: ". . . to order her to go into the king to implore his favor and to plead with him for her people" (Esther 4:8).

The request was simple. Esther was being asked to use her position as queen to save her people. Now, someone may say that God didn't ask Esther to do anything. The name of God isn't even mentioned in the book of Esther, it was Mordecai who asked her. No, God used Mordecai as His mouthpiece, but the request originated with God, and we're going to see that Esther recognized this fact.

The risk

At first glance, it seems pretty simple. "Esther, you're the queen of the Persian Empire. The king obviously likes you, and you've got some pull, so just get us out of this jam. Do some honey-nudging for us." But it *wasn't* that simple at all! In fact we find that Esther wastes no time in telling Mordecai that it wasn't that simple.

Then Esther spoke to Hathach and ordered him to reply to Mordecai: "All the king's servants and the people of the king's provinces know that for any man or woman who comes to the king to the inner court who is not summoned, he has but one law, that he be put to death, unless the king holds out to him the golden scepter so that he may live. And I have not been summoned to come to the king for these thirty days." (Esther 4:10–11)

The circumstances all looked negative and impossible. Being the wife of the king was largely ceremonial and positional, rarely intimate and relational, and she couldn't come and see the king anytime she wanted; she had to be summoned.

She hadn't been summoned by the highly volatile and unpredictable king for an entire month, a point she quickly raised with Mordecai. For whatever reason, in Esther's mind, her relationship with Ahasuerus was not at its best. It was a dangerous time to be asking huge favors.

Furthermore, the decree had originated with Haman, the king had only rubber-stamped it. Now, she was being asked to put her relationship with the king up against the king's relationship with Haman, a person he respected and admired enough to put in charge of his whole kingdom.

The king had thousands of beautiful women available for his every desire. But a dependable, savvy, and sharp advisor, who would take much of the burden of running the government and advising him, was hard to find. The odds were greatly against Esther. Besides, any decree from a Persian king was irrevocable. It was law! Even the king himself couldn't stop it now.

Asking the impossible

In her mind, what she was being asked to do was impossible. When you consider that *she* wasn't in imminent danger, you can easily see that the easy way out would have been to simply tell Mordecai, "No, sorry, I can't do that." It's obvious from her reply to Mordecai that her confidence in his plan was minimal. There were a million reasons why she shouldn't step out in faith, why she shouldn't step out of her comfort zone and get involved. As is so often the case, however, God didn't wait until Esther felt ready. He called on her to serve Him when things were all up in the air, when it seemed very risky, and when she didn't *feel* prepared.

She had no way of knowing at that moment that this is what God had been preparing her for all her life, that He had opened every door to get her to this point, and that she *was* ready.

Pandora's box

We've all been there, haven't we? How often do we view our greatest moments of fear and dread as opportunities to be used by God? Who might we bring relief and deliverance to? How many moments will God give us?

We are surrounded by powerless people in danger in many different ways. They are unable to help or protect themselves.

Most of us have been put into contact with such people. Maybe it's an abused or ignored child, a battered wife, a young teenager who is the target for the neighborhood children. Or could it be that those we know are in darkness, ignorant of the light that Jesus brings? Does God want to use us to pierce their darkness and allow His good news to work its power in them as it did in us?

As a pastor I am privy to countless human situations in which the intervention of just one person in a tangible way could bring deliverance or relief.

However, invariably there will be negative circumstances to consider. Helping someone in genuine need is often tantamount to opening Pandora's box. When I came across a homeless family in our town who simply asked for food, it was easy to say yes. But when their car broke down, and other needs turned up, it became more complicated, more involved. I discovered that I enjoy helping when it is neat, simple, and quickly over. It is less attractive when it becomes messy, complicated, tedious, and drawn out.

Just ordinary people

Esther's responsibility was going to reach far beyond the initial request she would make of the king. She would become more involved than she probably thought she would. Such is the job God often calls us to. Yet, He makes no apology, and He isn't worried about our feelings of not being ready for all this.

At times we want to remind God that we're not heroes, we're just ordinary people. We're not designed for this kind of work. Esther hadn't grown up in the royal court; she was just an ordinary Hebrew maiden.

I am reminded of Latricia Reese, the seven-year-old girl swept by raging flood waters into a Houston storm drain. She plunged several levels underground, twice falling more than six feet before reaching out and clutching a crack in the wall. In all she fell thirty feet down into a sewer drain.

The fire department diving team was called out, but they refused to enter the swift waters, saying, "It's just too dangerous." The police department divers also refused to enter the raging waters. She was finally rescued the following morning, not by professionals, but by two construction workers.

A young child was holding on for life in the pitch darkness of a sewer drain, till she finally saw a light. Two ordinary people saved her life. Did they consider themselves ready for what they ended up doing? God uses ordinary people, ordinary people willing to walk directly into the jaws of negative circumstances.

However we're going to see that God was going to ask her to take an even more difficult step.

Be Willing to Sacrifice All You Have Gained

This situation reminds me of the familiar story of the chicken and the pig discussing what to have for breakfast. The chicken says, "Let's have eggs and bacon. I'll bring the eggs and you bring the bacon." The pig declined, reasoning, "You're only being asked to make a contribution, I'm being asked to make a real sacrifice."

God wasn't asking Esther to make a mere contribution to a cause, He was asking her to make a real sacrifice, to put it all on the line.

But even more than that, she was being asked to give up all she had gained. Only several years ago she was a nobody, a conquered Jewish female in a male-dominated society, yet today she was the queen of the Persian Empire, enjoying both power and privilege. To do what Mordecai asked would be to risk all that. Mordecai knew that Esther was dealing with these issues, we can see it in his reply: "If you remain silent at this time, relief and deliverance will arise for the Jews from another place and you and your father's house will perish. And who knows whether you have not attained royalty for such a time as this?" (Esther 4:14).

Mordecai goes right to the heart of the matter telling Esther in essence, "You're in the lap of luxury right now, you've got all you could dream of, and you probably don't want to risk that. But don't just assume that God has given you this great job, position, wealth, and lifestyle simply for your personal enjoyment.

"You may assume that everything you have and enjoy was meant for only your benefit and satisfaction, but could it be that God gave you all these blessings to accomplish *His* purposes? Has it ever occurred to you that attaining this position was never meant entirely for your benefit, but so that you could be used by God for *His* purposes?"

What a waste

In 1904, William Borden, heir to the Borden Dairy fortune, graduated from a Chicago high school a millionaire and a Christian. His parents gave him a trip around the world. Traveling through Asia, the Middle East, and Europe, he developed a burden for the world's hurting people. Writing home, he told his family, "I'm going to give my life to prepare for the mission field."

When he made this decision, he wrote in the back of his Bible two words: "No Reserves." Turning down high-paying job offers after graduating from Yale University, he entered two more words in his Bible: "No Retreats."

After completing studies at Princeton Seminary, Borden sailed for China to work with Muslims, stopping first in Egypt for some preparation. While there he was stricken with cerebral meningitis and died within a month.

We would be tempted to say, "What a waste!" But it wasn't a waste in William's eyes. For in his Bible, underneath the words "No Reserves" and "No Retreats," he had written the final words: "No Regrets."

God often asks us to be willing to sacrifice all we have gained—a difficult step. Are we willing to sacrifice all we have gained? This was Esther's response:

Esther told them to reply to Mordecai, "Go, assemble all the Jews who are found in Susa, and fast for me; do not eat or drink for three days, night or day. I and my maidens also will fast in the same way. And thus I will go in to the king, which is not according to the law; and if I perish, I perish." So Mordecai went away and did just as Esther had commanded him. (Esther 4:15–17)

Unknown to her, this was her moment of destiny, the moment for which God had prepared her. But keep in mind that she had no way of knowing it.

Completely afraid, but fully prepared

What was that morning like for Esther? Weak, possibly dizzy from lack of food and sleep, emotionally drained from the immensity of the step she was about to take, Esther must have been exhausted. And that was the strength she had to face the greatest crisis of her life.

Esther was fully prepared for the worst. She understood that taking a step of faith does not always mean that what you want will happen. But faith believes that while some situations seem like they are destined for evil, God can turn them for good.

Esther must have known the stories of Joseph and Daniel in the Old Testament. Now, she was in Joseph's and Daniel's position. Faith was never designed, as some today teach, to remove you from situations like calamity, sickness, and bankruptcy, but to empower you to overcome those situations. Faith carries us *through* trials, not out of them.

There is probably no greater test of our faith than when God asks us to be willing to give up all that we hold dear in this world.

Contents under pressure

For years I was privileged to lead a singles' ministry in a church. In this sexually permissive age, those young people faced horrendous pressure to be sexually active.

When you add to this pressure the deep loneliness and desire for romantic love that rages within them, at times the issue of sexual purity comes to a boiling point. They often face terribly difficult decisions—either succumb to the sexual pressure of the one they love or risk losing him or her forever.

I have sat with wonderful young Christian women in tears, struggling with this decision, and with what they were afraid it would cost them. They would explain how they had waited years for the right one to come along, and just when they were sure they had found him, they found themselves faced with losing the one they cherished, all to remain faithful to Christ.

These would prove to be some of the hardest decisions they would ever make in their lives. They had no way of knowing whether their stand for sexual purity would cost them their relationships or not. They wanted some divine reassurance that if they did the right thing they would not lose out, but there wasn't any. They were forced, as we all are, to try to make sense out of the silence of God.

Some of them made the right decisions, and did not lose their relationships, but instead gained renewed respect. Others made the right decision and it cost them their relationships, and there was deep hurt for awhile. But later, for some, when God brought along men who loved Christ, men also committed to sexual purity, they saw God's shadow.

Others, tragically, made the wrong decision, and found that it cost them not only their purity, but also their relationships in the long run. In succumbing sexually they did not gain love, they only lost respect.

But in each case they were asked to be willing to sacrifice all they had gained, and there are times when God asks that of us.

Only God could ask something like that

Have you found yourself in just such a situation? Have you arrived at the place you've always dreamed of being, just to find that God seems to be asking you to risk all you have gained?

Maybe you've been lonely, looking for a spouse, and after a terribly long wait, you have found someone you feel is the answer. But he or she is making demands of you which you know God forbids. It is in these times that the words of Jesus become less abstract, and more personal than ever. "If anyone comes to Me, and does not hate his own father and mother and wife and children and brothers and sisters, yes, and even his own life, he cannot be My disciple" (Luke 14:26).

There are some things I wouldn't do for anyone but my wife or my children. If anyone else asked, it would be easy to say no, but my love for my family causes me to do it. No one but God could ask us to do some things, only He has the right to.

But, have you noticed that when we are in difficult situations, and doing the right thing is hard, it seems that with each passing day the decision to do the right thing gets harder and harder, not easier and easier. We see that also in Esther's case because God asks her ultimately to take probably the most difficult step.

Resist Last-Minute Temptations to Change Course

As she walked toward the inner court, her heart must have been pounding so hard that she thought everyone could see it through her dress. Her hands were probably cold and clammy, and her mouth dry.

Then, she must have seen Ahasuerus conducting the business of the empire, ordering things to be done with commanding authority. She hadn't seen him in a month. Was he mad at her? Were these her last minutes on earth, or did God have other plans? What *were* God's plans, anyway?

Then came the moment when the king must have noticed her, unbidden, a complete breach of court etiquette. And there she stood, her fragile life in his powerful hands.

Did thoughts of Vashti's decline flash through her memory? Vashti had only been deposed; Esther could be killed for what she was attempting. Was Ahasuerus already having a bad day? Was he in a foul mood? How the questions must have raced through her mind! Her eyes must have been riveted on only one thing, the scepter. Would it be raised?

It happened when the king saw Esther the queen standing in the court, she obtained favor in his sight; and the king extended to Esther the golden scepter which was in his hand. So Esther came near and touched the top of the scepter. (Esther 5:2)

Can you imagine her excitement, her sense of relief, at having gotten past this point? Remember, she was playing Russian roulette with her life by just walking a few yards into the inner court. But coming from a three-day fast and an intense time of prayer, she must have looked drained and worried. Concern and worry must have lined her face, and the king evidently had noticed, for we read: "The king said to her, 'What is troubling you, Queen Esther? And what is your request? Even to half of the kingdom it will be given to you' " (Esther 5:3).

He knew that for her to come at risk of her own life it must have been a serious matter, so he willingly puts aside his previous business and focuses his attention entirely on her. His love for her had not grown cold, in fact his tender response to her indicates that he was still in love with her. And then it came! The temptation! The incredible last-minute temptation to bail out. "Even to half of the kingdom it will be given to you."

Upping the ante

It wasn't bad enough that she was being asked to give up all she had gained, she was at the last minute offered more. While the phrase, "even to half of the kingdom it will be given you," should not be taken literally, it was still a generous offer. It would be like saying, "I love you so much, I'll give you whatever your heart desires."

Persian kings could be very generous, granting fortunes with just a word. Ahasuerus had evidently been able to deduce from her unannounced appearance that something very important was on her mind, and he wanted her to know that no reasonable request would be denied her. He was saying, "I love you," the best way he knew how.

How frequently we encounter this same temptation. We finally summon the courage to do what we know we have to, and instead of the decision getting easier, it gets harder. Wouldn't it have been tempting to have simply asked for some extravagant material comfort, or a long vacation until the situation blew over?

This is one of the most effective tools that Satan has in his arsenal. If we are willing to sacrifice what we have been given, take a stand and follow God no matter what the price, he often simply ups the ante. Satan never walks away quietly in defeat; he increases the pressure. He wants to know what our price tag might be.

We can expect last-minute temptations to change course, to abandon difficult decisions that were born of faith.

Scaling Satan's bluff

A good friend of ours had just read an article from a homosexual scientist proposing that it was genetics, and not human nature and sin, that leads people into homosexuality. Knowing that the Bible clearly teaches homosexuality is a choice, and a sin, she felt heavily burdened to send a letter to the Opinion section of the newspaper giving the scriptural viewpoint. She was not mean-spirited or vindictive, she simply took a stand for biblical truth.

It was a hard decision I'm sure. She knew that taking a stand might lead to criticism, but she was willing to take the heat. Her letter was printed, and she did receive heat, but far more than she expected.

True to form, since Satan couldn't stop her from taking a stand and sending the letter, he simply upped the ante. She soon began receiving letters at her home—angry, violent, and threatening letters. Since her address was not printed in her letter to the editor, she knew someone had gone to great lengths to find it. She feared for her safety, and that of her family. Don't you think at that point she was tempted to throw in the towel and say, "Well, I'm certainly not going to do *that* again. Let someone else fight these battles."

She didn't. While her fear was real, she knew she had done the right thing. She has since written on many subjects supporting moral values and biblical truth, a lonely voice speaking the truth, regardless of the cost. The same thing will happen in our lives. Satan attempts a gambler's bluff, but it can be a real temptation.

Esther resisted this temptation. In spite of the fact that Esther did not *feel* ready to take the step God asked of her, in spite of the fact that all the circumstances *looked* bad, in spite of the fact that *human reason* might say don't do it, she knew God was asking her to take these steps. She did not know what the outcome would be. Remember her words, "If I perish, I perish"?

This is definitely not the power of positive thinking at its best here. She'd simply resigned herself to doing what God had asked of her, regardless of the cost. She was willing to lose it all because she had come to the realization that God was the One who had given it to her, and He had done so with His purposes in mind, not just hers. This was what Mordecai had reminded her of. She was first, a servant of God; she was second, queen of Persia.

Faith works best in the worst of times

It's funny, but often very true, that in the difficult decisions of our lives we don't struggle as much with what is right as with the price tag associated with doing what is right. We just can't believe God would ask us to do what it seems He is asking us to do.

What are the difficult steps in your life right now? They have probably already come into your mind. As difficult as it may seem, it is true that faith operates best in the worst of times. There are times in our lives when God will unapologetically ask us to walk by faith into the jaws of negative circumstances, to be willing to sacrifice all we have gained, and to resist any last-minute temptations to change course. These are the worst of times for us, but they can be the best of times for our faith.

"He can't want me to stay in this marriage, I'm tired and my love is gone. It will just never work out, it's too much to expect. Since God wants me happy, and I'm not happy, He must want me to get a divorce."

"He can't expect me to stay pure sexually, the temptations are just too great. I'll never make it. If I don't give in, I will lose this person's love, and I know I will never find someone this special again."

"He can't expect me to cut back on my hours at work and give them to my family. I could lose my job! Besides, if I want to get ahead, I have to keep pushing. This just isn't the time, maybe someday . . ."

"He can't expect me to forego my career and stay home and raise my children. How will we live? How could I face my friends? Where would *I* find fulfillment?"

"He can't expect me to retain my integrity in the work force, I'll be left behind. They'll chew me up and spit me out. I've got to play by their rules to get ahead in this world. I'll be good everywhere else!"

"He can't expect me to give up my chemical dependency, it's impossible. There's no way I could handle my problems and pain without pills; I don't have the strength."

"He can't expect me to carry this baby to term, it will ruin my life, slow me down, and complicate my life. Besides, he will leave me if I have the baby. God has to understand that abortion is the only option I've got."

"He can't expect me to . . ."—you fill in the rest!

It seems so unreasonable, but in the end it's the very process God uses to mature and strengthen us, and often to bring greater blessing into our lives than ever before.

You don't *have* to feel ready to be obedient, circumstances don't *have* to seem favorable, temptation doesn't *have* to be removed in order to do what God is calling you to do.

In short, God doesn't need to speak or intervene in a miraculous way. The stage has been set, the necessary preparations have been made in our lives, and we are *ready*. His audible voice isn't necessary because He has already intervened. The great question is, do we believe this?

In the drama of our lives, God occasionally asks us to play some difficult parts. He simply asks us to trust Him that the part He has picked out for us is one He knows we can play.

The rewards for taking these difficult steps are rarely seen quickly, only over time. Invariably there will be times when you will wonder, especially if circumstances go from bad to worse, whether these difficult steps you took were really worth it.

Mordecai must have wondered as well when the blessing would arrive for the difficult steps he had taken, steps only God could have seen.

Five

Struggling in Obscurity

Every several years our world goes through a ritual of un-precedented proportion. Gathering around our televisions in major cities, small towns, deserts, jungles, snowbound hamlets, in any and every place imaginable, from virtually every spot on this great globe, we prepare to witness the competition of Olympic athletes.

Yet in reality, this is the end of their story, not the beginning. All of the thousands upon thousands of hours of practice; of falling, spraining, twisting, bruising; of discouragement and sweat and tears and losing and winning have brought them to the Olympics.

But for some, all that time and investment come down to a ten-second sprint, or a two-minute charge down a snow-packed hill, or a three-minute performance on the ice-skating rink. And for most there will be no second chance. This is it, their moment to perform what they have been practicing over and over again. The window of opportunity is open briefly, then slams shut.

Olympic moments

Everything they have invested their lives in, everything that has consumed them for years, finally comes down to one decisive and brief Olympic moment. Many of them will measure their entire lives by this one performance.

Sports commentators have named these times "Olympic moments," and if we think about it, life also provides us such moments.

Godliness, cultivated and nurtured continually in spite of occasional failure, discouragement, setbacks, opposition, and obscurity, often culminates one day in a momentous and all-too-sudden performance.

Thrust unsuspectingly into the spotlight after lifetimes of obscurity, we discover that our entire lives may be measured by our performances at this time.

And like those brave Olympians, we don't always come to these moments on the heels of victory and strength. Perhaps that's why we tend to cheer a little louder and harder for those who have overcome incredible obstacles to arrive at these places.

We may diligently practice all the godly character traits that God desires and yet still find the results in our lives to be disappointing. We look for the promised medal ceremony and lose heart when it seems there won't be any.

When life blooms slowly

It is here we learn a valuable truth for spiritual growth:

*The seeds of righteousness often take
longer to bloom than we expect them to.*

We discover, much to our chagrin, that the divine formula for blessing, trusting and obeying, is not the instant recipe we supposed it to be. In the same way that Olympic champions don't win medals for all their races or performances, neither do we.

And when God seems silent during these periods, we are tempted to question the value of the seeds we took such pains to plant and to nurture, seeds of fidelity, integrity, faithfulness, purity, and honesty.

We find instead that the divine formula for blessing often simmers and brews in extended silence. Like waiting anxiously for a seed to grow, we become impatient and despair that it will ever sprout. But the germination of God's working in our lives occurs in a realm invisible to our sight, which makes the waiting, at times, almost unbearable.

Yet, strangely, it is this fact that causes God's silence to make sense. When we ask God to be working, He surely is, but only by faith can we be certain of it.

We see proof of this in the life of Mordecai. While there are several crowning Olympic moments in Mordecai's life we will look at, I'd like to take us first to the one we identify with most readily.

When the edict manipulated by Haman goes out, and the extermination of the entire race is legislated and approved, we find Mordecai writhing in the agony of defeat.

When Mordecai learned all that had been done, he tore his clothes, put on sackcloth and ashes, and went out into the midst of the city and wailed loudly and bitterly. (Esther 4:1)

Can we understand the depth of his bitterness? In his life we will see that he had planted beautiful and delightful seeds of righteousness and blessing, but it seemed that all he would harvest for his effort would be thorns, weeds, and death. It was a truly human, truly bitter moment for Mordecai.

But to truly comprehend the depth of Mordecai's pain, we must go back and witness the seeds of righteousness that he had so gallantly and hopefully planted years earlier— seeds of righteousness he must surely have planted with the expectation that they would someday bloom.

Planting the seeds of righteousness

Can we go back to the day he heard little Hadassah (Esther's Hebrew name), his uncle's daughter, had suddenly lost her parents? Was she just a baby, crying, unable to care for herself? Or, was she a precious young girl of three or five or eight years of age with tears of loss and pain streaking her face, alone in a hostile world?

How alone and vulnerable she must have seemed to him. With compassion he took Hadassah and gave her all the benefits and privileges of his own family, making her his daughter. She became precious to him. Surely there would be blessing in store as Mordecai sowed seeds of compassion and care in this little girl's life. Surely God had a purpose in it.

As we turn to another page in Mordecai's life we find him sitting in his position at the king's gate, overhearing two officials plotting the king's death. He quickly informs Esther, who tells the king what Mordecai had said, and the king's life is saved. Planting seeds of righteousness and loyalty, he surely must have believed that God would cause these seeds to grow as well. God would see and He would bless.

A short time later a new prime minister was appointed to the king, a man named Haman. The command had gone out from the king that everyone was to bow down to Haman.

Maintaining his convictions and refusing to compromise, he plants a seed he surely must have expected God to cause to bloom in righteousness. Surely God would see, surely He would act!

Later, after Mordecai hears that his unwillingness to bow to Haman has sentenced his entire people to death, he steadfastly refuses to bow to Haman. Under sentence of death himself, he clings to his faith.

How many of us, when we are threatened with hostility or a significant and painful loss for sharing our faith or dealing righteously with others, will continue the practice that got us into trouble? He resisted the urge so prevalent today to find a loophole. And another seed of righteousness is planted with the hope and belief that God would see, God would act!

Even amid the silence of God and under the shadow of death, Mordecai refuses to give in.

Finally, we witness Mordecai taking probably his most difficult step of all, deciding to ask Esther to intercede on behalf of her people, and to let her race be known. This would be at risk of her life.

Trusting God with your own life is one thing, but trusting God with the life of your precious daughter is quite another. He loved and cared for Esther deeply, but he knew that God had a plan for her life. He bravely plants a final seed of righteousness, showing that he was willing to give up and sacrifice all that was precious and dear to him, his job, his life, and yes, even his beloved Esther, all for his faith in God.

Surely God would water this greatest seed of righteousness and bless it, and cause it to bloom. But before we start looking for Mordecai in the winner's circle, let's remember that all the early indicators were that his seeds of righteousness were all coming up weeds!

Deceptive early growth

What was the initial consequence of his loving care of his little Hadassah? She was wrenched from his faithful and holy Jewish home and influence and protection, and prepared to fulfill the sensual desire of a pagan king for a night of sexual ecstasy.

Had he cared and loved and nurtured Hadassah so that she could be given into the hands of an unpredictable king as a prize in his harem? The seed of righteousness he had so lovingly planted appeared to have bloomed into a hideous and ugly weed. How could this be?

And let's consider the plot Mordecai uncovered against the king's life. For his loyalty, Mordecai got—*nothing!* Apparently no mention is made of it, nor any indication given that the king even acknowledged his part in this rescue. Like planting beautiful pansies and being rewarded with crabgrass.

And what of his valiant and uncompromising stand for his faith in God by not bowing to Haman? What did that seed of righteousness become? The sentence of death upon his people, courtesy of *his* unwillingness to yield.

Seeds and weeds: ignoring the connection

This all brings us to an interesting spiritual truth that can help us make some sense out of the silence of God, and gain heart when all the wrong things start growing in our lives. While we're busy planting seeds of righteousness *in* our lives, Satan is just as busy planting weeds of unrighteousness *around* our lives.

Satan seeks to discourage us by planting weeds of calamity so close to our lives that we mistake them for the real seeds of righteousness that God is still germinating. If he can get us to believe that the weeds are the only harvest we're going to have, perhaps we'll neglect the seeds of righteousness, grow impatient, and stop cultivating faithfulness, integrity, and personal purity.

True harvest

While the weeds grew quickly and loomed over Mordecai's life, they had no roots, and just as quickly died leaving only the dried husks as reminders of their presence.

Pushing away the ugly weeds and blooming so magnificently that all memory of them is soon forgotten, the seeds of righteousness planted by Mordecai years earlier begin their long-promised bloom with breathtaking grandeur and beauty.

His precious Esther is protected and blessed, and she finds favor with the king. Ahasuerus suddenly remembers Mordecai's unrewarded heroic deed on his behalf; Haman's tragic end becomes inevitable.

This point deserves special attention. While it seemed the deed had been forgotten, God had made sure it was. Why? Because when King Ahasuerus found out about Haman's treachery, he probably felt a deep sense of betrayal. Haman was obviously his most trusted advisor, maybe the closest thing he had to a best friend. How could he find someone to trust now?

History provided him with the perfect answer. Had not Esther and Mordecai saved his life? It would be perfectly natural for Ahasuerus to then turn to Mordecai, someone history had shown he could trust with his very life. This seed of righteousness had to bloom later to accomplish its perfect plan. This can give us encouragement if our seed of righteousness is a late-bloomer.

Haman, the man who loved to hate Mordecai, loses his position to him instead, and is forced to lead Mordecai in a procession of the greatest honor and privilege. Ah, could Mordecai finally begin to smell the sweet aroma of vindication?

The Jews are saved, empowered by God to win a great victory over their enemies, and Mordecai goes from being a goat to smelling like roses.

What is interesting is that we are told that Mordecai became "greater and greater." In fact, the very last verse of the book of Esther casts its spotlight not on the queen, but on the once obscure and struggling Mordecai.

Mordecai the Jew was second only to King Ahasuerus and great among the Jews, and in favor with the multitude of his kinsmen, one who sought the good of his people and one who spoke for the welfare of his whole nation. (Esther 10:3)

This was the seed he had planted, and this is what grew—eventually!

This was the same man who had done the right things for the right reasons, and yet who had to endure one setback after another. He was not an overnight star, but one who practiced godliness when no one would see it, or pay attention to it, even when it threatened to cost him every-thing he cherished most: Esther, his people, and his life.

When is the payoff?

The application to our own lives is obvious. If we plant seeds of righteousness in hopes of seeing overnight fruit, we're going to be *disappointed.* If we plan on seeing God answer all our prayers and bless all our actions immediately, we are setting ourselves up for disappointment. Struggling in obscurity is part and parcel of the Christian calling, in fact it may *be* the Christian calling, but seeds of righteousness will bloom *eventually!*

This answers the burning question we all ask ourselves at one time or another, but rarely out loud: "When does doing the right thing pay off? When will things start going for me instead of against me? If God is out there, why doesn't He answer me, and get me out of this jam? Doesn't He know I'm on His side?"

Doing the right thing for a very long time without any external confirmation or blessing can tax our patience. In God's silence we can be tempted to deduce that God has forgotten to bless, or has no intention of doing so.

When we have to wait faithfully in the shadows, doing right simply because it is right, and making sacrifices so painful it amazes us that God allows it, we need to know that the seeds of righteousness we have planted will indeed bloom.

Hidden in these truths are some practical pointers for planting seeds of righteousness in our own lives that may be of some help, beginning with:

Be careful what you plant!
We reap what we sow.

We sow many things in our lives rather hastily and thoughtlessly, without much consideration for what we're planting and what might grow as a result. The less thought we give to our actions, the more likely we are to be planting weeds in our lives.

Coming home tired and discouraged from a hard day's work at jobs we dislike, we are prone to sow seeds of anger, impatience, and intolerance. We don't even have to work on it, our reaction is automatic. Quick words, short tempers, and soon our spouses and our children are scurrying for cover and for some way to survive our cutting remarks. But one day we find spouses and children have learned to shoot back in self-defense, and our homes become war zones.

It doesn't take much to grow weeds, but have you ever tried to get rid of them once they've taken root? Seeds of anger, bitterness, lust, envy, jealousy, and pride easily take root in us, in our sinful natures, and once planted they can quickly take over our lives.

Our sinful nature provides us bulging bags of seed, readily available and easily within reach, but seeds of righteousness are more precious, more rare, and require care and cultivation. You can throw weed seeds anywhere, in the most inhospitable environments, and they will grow quickly, but not seeds of righteousness.

There is nothing careless about the planting of seeds of righteousness. They take careful cultivation and preparation and nurturing, for righteousness is a more exotic plant, uncommon to our old nature, able to grow only in the soil of our new nature. Only a seed of righteousness, born of the Spirit, and regularly watered by the Word of God and prayer, will grow to maturity and bear fruit.

You cannot casually scatter seeds of truth, integrity, kindness, mercy, forgiveness, and love, and then abandon them and hope they will take root in your life. They must be cultivated.

Pruning too close

Not long ago, my wife and I became aware that we were both growing sharp and impatient with our children and their selfish behavior. We realized we were spending a great deal of our time telling them what they were doing wrong, and very little time telling them what they were doing right. While our children were regularly receiving the snips and cuts of the gardeners' sharp shears, they were being deprived of the necessary nutrients of encouragement and praise necessary for healthy growth.

After considerable prayer, my wife wisely created a chart that we placed on our family room wall. Inscribed on the chart were the words of Jesus in Mark 9:35, "If anyone wants to be first, he shall be last of all, and servant of all."

Each child has ten pouches. Every time our children act in an unselfish manner, or with kindness, or help someone, they are rewarded with a stick to place in their pouches. When all their pouches are full, they are rewarded with some special gift. While these treats aren't lavish, the change in our children's attitudes was literally immediate. They were no longer receiving only pruning for wrong behavior, now their kindness and goodness was receiving attention and being cultivated as well. We only wish we had thought of this earlier.

Beware! Weeds hide the progress of healthy plants.

A marriage planted in the best soil can still evidence problems. Children given a truly Christian home can still reject that upbringing. Confessing your faith can still get you fired, and maintaining your integrity can definitely cost you potential business.

Doing the right things, as we've seen in this chapter, is no guarantee that we will then be able to ride off happily into the sunset, singing, "Happy Trails." Sometimes the good guy does finish last—for awhile.

While we're patiently waiting for God to cause the seeds of righteousness we've planted to grow and then bloom in our lives, Satan is planting his own seeds around our lives.

If he can take a sore spot in our marriage relationships, or divert our children's attention with one of his alluring temptations, or incite our boss to fire us for our faith, or give the big contract to someone who's willing to lie or cheat, then maybe he can convince us that this is how it's always going to be.

Mordecai's great strength was his ability to look past the weeds and wait expectantly for the seeds of righteousness to bloom! So, expect the weeds, but don't mistake them for what you've planted.

Be patient! Righteousness blooms slowly.

There was a period in my life several years ago when all I could see for all the good things I had planted were tall weeds. I was surprised, confused, and deeply hurt. After all, I had expected something entirely different to be blooming. But in the midst of my confusion and misunderstanding, God spoke gently but powerfully to me from a seemingly innocuous little verse in Proverbs: "The path of the righteous is like the light of dawn, that shines brighter and brighter until the full day" (4:18).

You see, I've often watched the light of dawn appear, so I immediately understood the picture. At first, everything is black as night, until at some point the slightest faint hue appears on the horizon. It is so slight it is barely discernible.

But slowly, and here I need to emphasize the word *slowly,* it begins to spread. What is more, nothing on earth can stop it, it is inevitable. And soon the darkness is chased completely away and light is everywhere, filling every space with warmth and brightness, until it culminates in the fullness of sunshine at noon.

Growing up in an "instant" age, I had succumbed to the idea that everything should happen quickly, because, after all, *I'm waiting for it!* But those seeds of righteousness must first break open in the soil of our lives, and then fragile roots must begin pushing their way down through some very hard soil to find the necessary spiritual nourishment. Only then can the upward thrust begin and the results become visible to the eye.

God makes it plain that the progress of righteousness is a slow process, but He also makes it clear that it is a *sure* process; eventually it grows rapidly and becomes visible and apparent.

One of the marvels that fascinate me when I visit the High Sierras is the frequent sight of tree roots growing quite literally *through* granite. The tiny fragile seed that could be easily destroyed with a child's fingers eventually grows to have such force and pressure that even the rocks on the mountains cannot stop its inevitable progress. Piles of shattered rock lie nearby, mute evidence of the tiny seed's latent power.

So if you've planted and cultivated seeds of righteousness, stop looking at your watch, this is a slow process. But never stop waiting for and expecting the first signs of growth, because it will come, and no power of Satan can stop it.

*Be encouraged! Plants of
righteousness bloom continually.*

Not long ago our church invited a man from a parachurch organization to come and speak for a series of classes in our adult Sunday school.

While I was alone with him one Sunday, he told me how he had grown up in a fine Christian home, but had still rejected Christianity. He left home to join the military and spent the next ten years in unbelief. But finally, the seeds of righteousness planted by his faithful parents took root. The germination was complete. He not only came to Christ, but entered full-time ministry.

What must not escape our notice is that his parents had to endure the silent waiting as the germination of that planted seed of righteousness slowly worked down into his hardened heart, finally breaking through. But when it did, the seed began to bloom and bloom and bloom!

What a joy must fill their hearts as they witness their son being a light in others' darkness, walking with Christ, teaching the very gospel he had rejected for so long. Gone are the weeds, now only dry empty husks of memory. Instead, a tall sturdy tree stands before them, sending out more seeds continually.

Isn't this what we see in Mordecai's life? Wouldn't it have been the answer to his prayer, to the seeds he had planted, just to have his Esther safe and his people out from under the shadow of death?

But he was given more, much more. He was given a royal parade, courtesy of his most hated enemy. Besides, Mordecai assumed Haman's position and received all his earthly goods. Through this he gained new access to his beloved Esther.

So if you've planted the seed, be patient, the wait is going to be worth it. God may seem silent, but we know now that He is not inactive. Furthermore, our God doesn't just fill cups, He fills them to overflowing.

As Charles Spurgeon, the great nineteenth-century preacher once said, "Lettuces, radishes, and such garden crops are soon out of the ground and ready for the table— a month almost suffices to perfect them. But an oak requires long centuries to come to the fullness of its growth."[1]

Mordecai made the hard choices when he needed to, but little did he know what terrible decisions his precious Esther would one day need to make. She would not be spared this spiritual exercise. One generation would pass to the next the baton, but greater pressure and changes awaited her than even her guardian had endured.

---

1. Charles Spurgeon, *The Quotable Spurgeon*. Wheaton, Ill.: Harold Shaw Publishers, 1990, 250.

Six

When the Spotlight Hits

"I don't know!" These are three of the most frustrating words a pastor has to utter to someone who has sought him out for direction. And I know they are the three words the person seeking answers least wants to hear. Yet today I find myself using these three words far more frequently than I used to.

These three words underscore a pressing issue many Christians face: how to find the will of God without a road map.

No one ever asks me, "Is God really against immorality?" or, "Would God mind if I robbed a bank?" These are questions of direction for which it is easy to give guidance. No, I get questions of a much different variety. Questions like:

Should I take this new job offer?

Should I home-school?

Should we adopt a child, or trust God to eventually give us one, even though He hasn't so far?

Should we buy the new house or not?

Am I being called into full-time ministry?

Am I being called out of full-time ministry?

What college should I attend?

Should I marry this person?

Having been asked all these questions, and many more like them, I have had to honestly reply, "I don't know." While I can give advice, most people come seeking an authoritative answer, and I'm not able to give it. They really want to hear a "Thus sayeth the Lord" that will settle the issue, and I often simply give them more to think about, making their decision even more difficult.

I know my answers have been disappointing, but the reality is, there are a number of questions or issues we face in life that no one can answer except God, which makes His seeming silence so difficult to understand.

We ask God for direction, but no heavenly telegrams arrive, and we feel we're all alone. We are sure God has a specific thing He wants us to do in this situation, but He hasn't seen fit to let us in on it.

There is so much at stake that we just know a wrong decision will mean years and years of heartache and trouble. But what do we do? What do we consider when making such decisions? We need look no further than Esther, who faced the same predicament.

Let's return to the pivotal moment in the story when Mordecai confronts Esther with Haman's wickedness and urges her to take a stand.

Do not imagine that you in the king's palace can escape any more than all the Jews. For if you remain silent at this time, relief and deliverance will arise for the Jews from another place and you and your father's house will perish. And who knows whether you have not attained royalty for such a time as this? (Esther 4:13–14)

What thoughts and emotions must have raged in Esther as she listened to Mordecai's gentle rebuke? Did the lessons of her youth, the words of the law of God spoken long ago to her by Mordecai, filter back into her heart and mind?

How far away that life must have seemed by now. She was far from the sights and sounds and people that would remind her of her faith. Everywhere Esther went there were statues and temples to Marduk and other pagan gods. Scenes of pagan worship and life, rampant in the Persian capital, must have so dominated her senses that the truths she had learned and believed as a young girl would seem like distant fading memories.

Polar bears in Bermuda

Many of us are forced to live and work in similar circumstances. In the situations in our lives, the Bible and its truths are as foreign as polar bears in Bermuda. Our senses are bombarded daily and continually with reminders that we are strangers, exiles, fish swimming upstream in a downstream world. We are outvoted, outnumbered, often mistrusted, or even disliked. And that's on our good days!

Did Esther blink? Did she waiver for a moment in her response to Mordecai? It is obvious that she was hesitant, and less than eager about Mordecai's suggestion.

In retrospect we mustn't be too hard on Esther when we consider her hesitancy. Her decision would not be an easy one. There was likely a period of time between Mordecai's challenge and Esther's response as Esther considered the implications of her decision.

As she fingered her priceless clothing and jewelry and walked on the marble floors and along the elegant corridors of the royal palace brilliantly adorned in gold; as she pondered her lavishly extravagant and comfortable lifestyle, safely protected by the royal guard, with royal attendants who bowed and catered to her every whim, was the decision she had to make really that simple?

She was being asked to risk losing everything, all for the sake of millions of people she had never seen, and from whom she may have felt far removed in the royal Persian palace.

The sound of silence

And Mordecai had put his finger right on the heart of the matter, with one single solitary word, *silence*. To ensure her own safety and privilege all she had to do was nothing; if she remained quiet she would probably remain safe.

There were no Jeremiahs or Ezekiels or Isaiahs who would prick her conscience or reveal the will of God to her. There was no place she could find the answer to her situation. It was unique. In the single greatest crisis of her life, with so much at stake, silence was the only sound she heard.

Ever been there? Maybe you're there right now. You are on the verge of one of the most important decisions of your life and you find you must make it all alone. While others would like to help, you find that the decision you must make is a lonely one. What is worse is that there seems to be no specific passage in the Bible telling you exactly what to do. Your situation is unique. In this most important moment of your life you find God is silent.

Road map or compass?

In these moments, what we seek most is a detailed road map, specific and detailed directions on exactly what we're supposed to do next, leaving nothing to chance. But in those moments we discover that God doesn't hand out road maps, He instead hands us a compass. It soon becomes obvious that God is more concerned that we're headed in the right direction than that we have all the details of our future. He knows that with the compass we will be far more attentive to His guidance and leading.

Esther was alone with just four things to consider in the most difficult and pivotal decision of her life. And when God is silent on the major issues of our lives, we are often alone with these same four realities.

1. The knowledge of how God has worked in our past

The poignant words of her beloved Mordecai must have echoed over and over again in her memory, "Who knows whether you have not attained royalty for such a time as this?" could her heart have escaped the almost too obvious implication?

The moving of God in her past was undeniable. She had once been an orphan girl from a conquered people. From that place God had thrust her into the greatest position of honor and wealth and power a woman could attain in the world of that day. Could she have escaped the gnawing question of why? With all that was at stake, the questions of *why me?* and *why now?* must have seemed almost blatantly obvious.

Being in an uncomfortable position does not mean you're not exactly where God wants you for the moment. Was Joseph comfortable when he was sold into slavery, or cast into Pharaoh's prisons? Was Daniel comfortable when he was forcibly removed from his homeland and forced to serve in his conqueror's courts? Would either of them have chosen this path themselves? The answer is an obvious one, but so is the point. They were right in the middle of God's will.

How has God moved in your past? Often when we have difficult decisions to make, the knowledge of how He has worked in our past can be helpful in determining what we need to do now. Can you see that He has moved you into places where you needed to be, and allowed you to experience things you needed to experience? All of these experiences become the building blocks for helping us discover what God has prepared us for today.

Can't God spread the blessings around a little?

When I was younger I used to wonder why God allowed me to go through all the pain He did. By the time I was sixteen I had been through three broken homes. Yet I lived in a neighborhood where all of my good, close friends came from stable, two-parent, lifelong-marriage homes.

I couldn't understand it. It didn't seem fair, and I often got frustrated and angry. Why couldn't God spread the misery around just a little more, or better yet, why couldn't He spread the blessings around a little more? What had I done to deserve all this?

My friends slept well at night, secure in their loving homes. I was often kept awake by arguments. Other kids couldn't wait for their fathers to come home to spend time with them. I dreaded my dad's arrival. Other kids' parents would have been ecstatic if their children *wanted* to go to church and read the Bible. I did these things and found them used against me by my father, who ridiculed my beliefs.

That was what I thought when I was sixteen. Now over two decades have passed, and I have discovered something fascinating. God has used all of those experiences to prepare me to minister in a way I never could have otherwise. Divorce is rampant in southern California where I have been called to minister. When I speak to couples about divorce, I tell them my background and they listen. When they speak of pain, they know I am familiar with that pain. I am uniquely qualified to minister to these people.

Furthermore, I minister not out of a deficit, as one might suppose, but out of a surplus. These experiences were not designed to destroy me, but to strengthen me.

The view that never gets old

It is like two men who both move to a beautiful lakeside. Each has a view of the lake, and enjoys it. However, one of the men grew up around the lake, and it is a common sight and experience for him. For him the lake is a playground. The other man, however, lived for years in a desert, where water was scarce, and thirst a constant companion. Now both men enjoy the lake, but for different reasons. The man who was thirsty so much of his life never tires of gazing upon so much water. It never gets old with him, and it is a sight that constantly reassures him that his desert days are over.

Ask yourself which man is truly more grateful for the lake, and more likely to cherish it and appreciate it? Who is least likely to get tired of it and move away? It is the memory of where he has been that makes the lake so precious for the once-thirsty man.

Having looked at my past, I can say honestly that I would not have changed a thing. I would never want to do it again, but I wouldn't undo it either. I learned empathy, compassion, trust, and faith in ways I might never have otherwise.

In many decisions I have to make, the knowledge of how God has worked in my past has had a substantial impact. I never forget that God was doing exactly as He promised He would in my life, conforming me slowly, more and more, into the image of His Son.

But while the knowledge of how God has worked in my past is important and can be helpful in the decisions I must make today, it is, by itself, often not enough. Which is why, like Esther, we must also consider:

2. The position God has placed us in today

We must remember that Esther had never actively sought her position. From all the evidence, it appears that the situation was probably quite the opposite. Can we believe that a Hebrew girl of maybe thirteen, who had been raised by a God-fearing and faithful Jewish relative, would seek to be wrenched from her home and familiar surroundings, to be placed in a giant harem?

While she would technically be the king's wife, she would be only one of hundreds, and she might have to spend the rest of her life childless and, for all practical purposes, without a husband.

Are we to believe this is the life a God-fearing Hebrew maiden would choose for herself? Yet, she finds herself suddenly thrust into a position of great power and influence. *Esther finds herself in a position to do what no one else can.*

Catapulted into a position of prominence how could she have escaped the evidence of God's hand in it? Many of us find ourselves in the same position.

A position on a school board, an employer in a company, a pastor in a church, these and many others like them are positions where we are available to make a significant impact, having a platform from which to support or enact righteous reforms.

Not long ago I attended a college football game, and before the game a number of the players ran into the end zone, and there knelt and prayed as a group. It was wonderful to see that they recognized they had been given a platform, and they would use it to honor their King.

Certainly others were willing to publicly share their faith, but they weren't given the athletic ability, they weren't given the platform.

I think of highly successful business people who use their positions to share the claims of Christ with others, gaining an audience where others could not. I think of professional football and basketball players using their positions of visibility to glorify God. While they have an audience, they use it to share their faith.

Step up to the platform, please

What position has God placed you in today? You aren't there by accident, but by plan. When we have been blessed by God with material prosperity, or have achieved a comfortable station safely isolated from many of the needs and pains of life, it is tempting to pull up the bridge over the moat and insulate ourselves. We're finally safe and comfortable and are reticent to risk our positions, or to again enter the difficult fray of life.

But could it be that God has given you this platform for a reason? Can you hear the words of Mordecai echoing in your heart, "For such a time as this"?

Mordecai pointed out to Esther that a king's palace wouldn't be enough protection for her. He removed any false sense of security she might have been holding to.

Sometimes the decisions we have to make are made easier when we consider that God has placed us where we are today, and for a purpose.

What might that purpose be in your life? How might that knowledge guide a difficult decision you have to make? Often we are unhappy with where we are, always wishing we were somewhere else, doing something else.

But while this information is helpful, it also is not enough to make a decision on. There is yet another thing Esther had to consider:

3. The truths God has already spoken

While we have discussed at length God's silence in the book of Esther, we must not forget that God had already given Esther and Mordecai sufficient truth to guide them.

Not knowing God's will in a certain decision doesn't necessarily mean He has been silent, it may just mean we have yet to discover His directly revealed will through Scripture.

Only a little over a hundred years before Esther's experience, in the same city in which she now reigned as queen, a faithful Hebrew exile named Daniel had risen to power in a miraculous way. Had he not also risked death at the hands of a pagan ruler? In fact, much like Esther, to have escaped the threat of death he needed do only what Esther may have contemplated: nothing!

Daniel's habit of prayer had not gone unnoticed by his enemies. So they manipulated King Darius into issuing a decree that anyone who prayed to anyone but him during a certain month should be killed. The plan was simple, since Daniel had never made a secret of his prayer life.

Knowing full well the consequences of once again praying toward Jerusalem publicly, he could have chosen to skip prayer. He would certainly be able to help his people more if he were alive, rather than dead. Like Esther, like us, Daniel faced a difficult decision for which there was no specific precedent. Daniel wasn't given any specific directions, but from the Scriptures he had, he could surely discover God's heart.

Hadn't God delivered Daniel from the lion's den? And had Daniel any more specific information than Esther to rely on when he made his decision?

Were Solomon's words part of her prayers? "The king's heart is like channels of water in the hand of the LORD; He turns it wherever He wishes" (Proverbs 21:1).

Did she search the Scriptures? Did her heart search her memory for the truths that had been placed there when she was just a young girl? Was God truly being silent in this issue, or had He already spoken enough to give her the necessary direction? Often we are waiting for God to repeat something He has already said.

Flying blind

Are the Scriptures truly silent on the issue you face today? Is it possible that there are scriptural principles relevant to your dilemma?

My parents were both pilots, so I have been on countless flights, and before we ever took off they thoroughly examined the prevailing weather conditions along the entire route we planned to take. A responsible pilot wouldn't dream of looking up in the sky and saying, "Well, it looks clear here, I'm sure it will be fine where we're headed."

Yet, at times, that's exactly what we do with God's Word. We often make major decisions that will have ramifications far into the future on the basis of a casual perusal of Scripture. If we don't see anything at first glance that seems to address our issue, we often assume there is nothing there. More than one pilot has flown into bad weather for that reason, and more than one Christian has made an important decision while "flying blind."

No miner ever made his fortune from the gold he collected out of an easily approachable stream. The fortunes were made by those who determined to find the vein that gold came from, often necessitating boring into entire mountains, or deep underground. If we would find the nugget of God's will, we must not expect that it will always be lying out where we could stumble upon it, but we must understand that searching is in order. The reward is well worth the effort.

We are told to approach the Scriptures in a very specific fashion. *"Be diligent* to present yourself approved to God as a workman who does not need to be ashamed, handling accurately the word of truth"* (2 Timothy 2:15, italics added).

Not ashamed of what? Not ashamed of sloppy, inattentive, and hasty conclusions drawn from casual glances. A proper study of Scripture relevant to our decisions will provide a fine, solid, brick house. A hasty study produces houses of hay and twigs that are easily blown over and destroyed.

But while Esther's awareness of the Scriptures surely helped in her decision, there was one last thing that could not have escaped her attention.

4. The example of godly mentors

All her life Mordecai had been the one she had leaned on for guidance. When she was in the harem, Mordecai was there, visiting her daily to learn how she was holding up (Esther 2:11). He knew this whole experience would be new and foreign and strange to his little girl, brought up adhering to the law of God. His tender and devoted love for his adopted daughter was evident.

Asking Esther to place herself at risk must have been one of the hardest things Mordecai had ever done. Yet it was not self-preservation that motivated his actions, but a faith and belief that God would deliver His people. He knew that relief and deliverance could arise for the Jews from another place, but He must have been astutely aware of God's working behind the scenes to place Esther in a position of power.

When Esther looked around for a role model to follow, someone's footsteps to follow in, she didn't need to look far.

Hadn't Mordecai risked everything for the sake of righteousness and his faith in God? Was he asking any more from her than he had already given? It had not been a secret to her that Mordecai had risked danger by refusing to bow to Haman. Even after the edict, Mordecai had steadfastly refused to compromise his faith. Like Daniel, Hananiah, Mishael, and Azariah before him, he would honor his God no matter what the cost.

Who is your Mordecai?

There are those who have gone before us, and learned how to navigate the tumultuous waves and gale-force winds of indecision with righteousness and integrity. They've been there and done that. They are not perfect, but they are experienced.

When we are faced with difficult decisions, we need to ask ourselves who the Mordecais are in our lives. Who are the godly examples and experienced travelers who have trusted God to guide them through dangerous country with nothing more than a compass, and have come out safely on the other side?

A number of years ago, when I was experiencing a difficult situation in my pastorate, and was struggling with what to do, I called on such a Mordecai. My mentor had walked with God for years, and was a wealth of godly wisdom and experience. As young pastors are wont to do, I was considering leaving my church over the problems I was experiencing. I had lost my desire to minister, in fact, I was considering leaving the ministry altogether.

As a last resort, I had lunch with my mentor, and shared my frustration with him. He listened patiently and attentively. When I finished my story and stated dispiritedly, "I think I might need to leave"; his reaction startled me. Instead of picking up a Bible and reminding me of my calling, or trying to shame me into changing my mind, he simply asked me a question. "How long have you been at this church?" When I told him that I had been there three years, he smiled and leaned back and said gently, "Oh, no, Dan, this is just your time, everyone goes through it."

He then went on to explain that most of the pastors he knew had gone through the exact experience I was describing. It was almost a necessary rite of passage, a dark-tunnel experience that each pastor must go through alone. I was not unusual, in fact I was right on time. That single bit of advice from my Mordecai kept me in the ministry when I didn't want to be there. And later, when God revived my desire for ministry, I called him blessed.

Checking our compass bearing

Such is the value of the Mordecais in our lives. The Bible could never contain all the information we would need to tell us specifically what to do in every situation in life. That's why God has provided various means to determine His will. But He has given us compasses instead of road maps.

The Scriptures continually point us toward the heart of God. One catechism says, "The chief end of man is to glorify God." This is true north, our compass bearing.

A compass won't tell you what's ahead, but it will keep you always traveling in the right direction and will deposit you at your ultimate destination. In the decisions we need to make, have we considered what would most glorify God? In other words, have we checked our compass?

If we are truly seeking to glorify God, will God not lead us in the right direction in our decision making? Don't the Scriptures tell us this?

"Trust in the LORD with all your heart, and do not lean on your own understanding. In all your ways acknowledge Him, *and He will make your paths straight*" (Proverbs 3:5–6, italics added).

Be honest, doesn't that sound a lot more like a compass reading than a road map? In the difficult decision you're facing today, have you checked your compass reading? Have you made part of your decision-making process what will most glorify God in this situation?

In the pivotal points in our lives when we must discern the will of God in important issues, God fully intends to make His will known. But He makes His will known most often in the slow, natural, and certain process of unfolding circumstances.

Esther's decision was obviously based on a number of things she perceived to be true and relevant to her situation, including her past, her present, her mentors, and the Scriptures.

When all else fails, follow the directions

While God knows all along what He wants us to do and will ultimately lead us through various means toward that end, *He often reveals the next move without revealing the final solution.*

Like a set of directions we find in something we buy at a store, we are led step-by-step to assemble the product. If we follow the directions faithfully, we end up with a correctly assembled item.

The natural temptation, however, is to look at all the assorted parts and just try to figure out how they could ever possibly become a gas grill. We are tempted to start guessing at how it might work, and we get ahead of ourselves, or worse, despair of ever figuring it out and give up.

But as Esther demonstrates, it is possible to find God's will without a set of specific directions.

For those three days she must have agonized, prayed, cried, quit, begun again, worried, planned, changed her plans, and continued this process until she was able to make peace, and come to terms with her final decision. And this, friends, is real life. This is a real person struggling with the real issues of life in a real way.

This may be your moment, the time in your life when you have to make a hard decision, a pivotal decision that will affect the rest of your life.

I want to clarify that it is not my intention through this chapter to give an "If you do this, then God will specifically tell you what to do" approach. Rather, it is my intention to show simply that we all find ourselves in situations where we have to make critical decisions when we feel we have little to guide us.

I hope that you will be able to see that while God doesn't provide a detailed road map, He definitely gives us a compass. And I hope this understanding points you in the right direction!

Both Esther and Mordecai faced terrible odds in the steps of faith they took. Though they appeared to never waver in their actions, we wonder if there weren't times when God's silence gave them pause. Behind every brave and bold step of faith lies an often hidden and silent war, a war within.

In this war we struggle not with external forces but internal ones. But why has God allowed this situation to arise in the first place?

Seven

Answering the Critics

A precious friend of mine died recently. Actually, I knew her only for the last six years since she started attending our church. She was eighty-six years old when she died, and her gray hair and aged features stood out among the thirty-something congregation I minister to. But it was her faith that most captured my attention.

When she went home to be with the Lord, I performed the funeral service. While many tears were shed, including my own, it was a time of gladness and hope and joy, because we knew where she was.

One particularly poignant moment came when her granddaughter read a beautiful eulogy. It was full of faith and assurance of her grandmother's presence in heaven. Their relationship was close and deep, their bonds not only of blood, but of faith.

After the funeral we drove to the gravesite, and as we waited for the casket to be brought, the granddaughter walked up to me quietly and whispered, "Now, this is all true, right? All this stuff we're saying about Grandma is really true isn't it? She really is in heaven, right?"

"Yes, she really is," I assured her.

"I've always believed it, but now—I just couldn't imagine Grandma being anywhere else—I couldn't take it."

Far from being shocked or disturbed by her statements, I found them refreshingly honest. It is so easy to parrot comforting platitudes and familiar words when the loved one is someone elses, but when this is *your* loved one, your faith faces its greatest challenge. And the challenge comes not from outside, but from within.

The granddaughter's faith in Christ and the resurrection was rock solid, but had probably never before been challenged to such an extent. Never had this belief been of more importance to her.

Addressing the critic within

When what we've always said we believed is finally and genuinely put to the test, a struggle ensues. This struggle does not mean we have lost our faith, it means we are having to exercise our faith at a different level than before, and are having to expend a greater effort than before.

When we choose to ignore warning signs of pain and confusion, and attempt to simply go through the motions of our Christian faith without conviction, we lay a landmine in our own spiritual lives that we will one day stumble upon.

No, the dangerous criticism comes not from someone else, but from our own unasked, unspoken, but very real concerns about God's apparent timidity, powerlessness, and silence in a dangerous world filled with loud, powerful, and evil people.

We are under undeniable pressure, from our world and all the forces of hell, to reconcile the truth we believe about the power and righteousness and faithfulness of our God with our current precarious situations, where God, it *seems*, is a nonfactor.

The view from the gallows

When we think about this situation, we are reminded of Haman's ultimate solution for Mordecai: the gallows (Esther 5:9–14).

Evil men like Haman are promoted and given accolades and power, while proven, faithful men like Mordecai are given the brush. What gives?

The gallows provides us some answers, for from the height of the gallows we can gain perspective. If we think about it, the gallows was the culmination of two competing ideologies, one in rebellion to and one in submission to the authority of God. As such, it provides a valuable object lesson, one God doesn't want us to miss.

From our human vantage point, the gallows was for Haman the place of expectation, and for Mordecai, the place of execution. Both men were fervently and passionately committed to their beliefs, but there was only one gallows upon which to judge the consequences of those beliefs.

They hanged Haman on the gallows which he had prepared for Mordecai, and the king's anger subsided. (Esther 7:10)

This gallows is a mute reminder, a silent object lesson. From the gallows we can make several observations.

The Higher the Platform, the Greater the Visibility

There is probably no greater opportunity to display God's work than when He is challenged or ridiculed or berated. Each gauntlet thrown down provides a new chance for God to strengthen the faith of His people.

The gallows became a billboard upon which Haman intended to advertise his power. No one builds a gallows seventy-five feet high (fifty cubits) unless he is trying to make a statement (Esther 5:14). A gallows ten feet high would be just as effective.

Everyone in Susa would see whoever was hung upon it, and would be reminded that Haman was in control, and no one should try to stand in his way.

Ironically, in retrospect, we can see that Haman himself built, designed, and funded the billboard precisely to God's specifications. God wanted not just Mordecai but all in Susa to see His power. The gallows reminds us that God is preparing a witness for Himself, and He doesn't want anyone to miss it.

God's recent billboards

All along God was preparing the billboard. Have we been looking at God's billboards in our own time? Charles Colson reminds us of some recent examples.

If you want to see the power of the church when it's out of power, just look at recent events in Eastern Europe.

May Day, 1990. Moscow's Red Square. The usual May Day parade with tanks and missiles, all flaunting Soviet military might. But this year, something interrupts the extravaganza. A group of Orthodox believers bursts into the parade, carrying aloft a huge crucifix, which blocks out the posters of Marx and Lenin. As they pass before the Soviet leaders, the priests cry out, "Christ is risen."

Within months, the Soviet Union collapses. What toppled it? The faith of millions of believers who echo in their hearts, "Christ is risen indeed."

Come with me now to Romania. Laszlo Tokes is pastor of a fast-growing Reformed Church. The communist government moves to silence him by sending him into exile; but when police arrive, believers from all traditions—Orthodox, Catholic, and Protestant—form a human wall around his church. That religious protest inspires the entire population of Romania to rise up against government oppression. Within days, the communist dictatorship falls.

In Czechoslovakia, an obscure priest, Father Maly, is beaten for his witness to the Gospel, and dispatched to clean toilets in the Prague subway system. Yet, on that fateful night in December, 1989, it is Father Maly who leads 800,000 people in a peaceful revolution that overthrows the communists. After 70 years of communist oppression, the Church is victorious.

Then Colson puts all these events in perspective.

Let's put away our posters, lick our wounds, and then get down to the basic business at hand—building the church. Our political fortunes may wax and wane, but the Church remains forever.[1]

It is only natural to be frightened when we see evil men and women become powerful. We fear their power in our government and in our high courts, in our school boards and our universities, and in the media and the

---

1. Charles Colson, *The Southern California Christian Times* (March, 1993), 9.

movie industry. But fear becomes even more intense when we see such people become powerful in our homes and our workplaces. Are we living under fear of their power and platform, wondering why God allows these situations to continue?

We need to see that the ladders they are climbing are precarious. Although it may seem like they can't fall, and like nothing can stop them, the very height to which they attain often becomes the measure of their downfall. The greater their visibility, the greater the opportunity for God to display His power in an unmistakable way.

But there is another observation we can make from the gallows, one that we don't often consider in the panic of fear and confusion.

The Greater the Evil, the Greater the Deliverance

The gallows wasn't simply a picture of great deliverance, it was undeniably a picture of great judgment. Judgment, like deliverance, demands an audience—the larger the better.

God wants us to know the extent to which He can protect us. He wants to move us out of the safety and comfort of the hypothetical ivory towers we often live in and lock the door behind us. When we find ourselves facing a much greater danger than any we've faced before, and we are forced to put our hypothetical and theoretical beliefs about God's protection into practice.

When we say God is powerful, we must always have a comparison. Theoretically we say He is more powerful than anything, but when danger looms near to us, we just want to know that God is more powerful than this present danger.

In these times of severe testing, God graciously provides the comparison.

How can we know the extent to which God can protect us until we have first been threatened? Moses had Pharaoh, Daniel had Nebuchadnezzar and Darius, Joseph had his brothers and Potiphar's wife, Elijah had Ahab and Jezebel, and each of us has someone or something in our lives that God will use to teach us the extent to which He can protect us.

Where there is no evil ruler or dangerous and powerful person in our lives, all knowledge of God's saving power becomes strictly hypothetical and theoretical to us. God wants to make it practical in our lives. He is determined that we understand the extent to which He can be trusted, and these lessons come only through experience.

It is not His reluctance to use His power that keeps Him from coming to our rescue earlier, but often His very desire to make His power so evident that we can't miss it!

And from the gallows, we also see that:

Facing Death Through Faith Is a Victory

Mordecai and Esther knew their actions could lead to death; they'd made peace with that. Nothing could stop them, not even the shadow of death, or the sound of the hammering on the gallows.

Death, as a result of faith, can still be a victory. Either way, Mordecai and Esther's lives would have brought glory to God. God has called some of His servants to make the ultimate sacrifice. Mordecai's actions showed he was willing to make that sacrifice. Esther showed she was willing.

Hebrews 11 lists those stalwart servants of God who were willing to endure terrible suffering and deprivation solely because of their faith.

In these instances, faith *is* the victory! The critics can argue with some of the church's past actions, or stands, or beliefs, but they are silenced in the presence of a faith so strong that even the fear of death does not control its actions.

Being willing to live in harm's way

All of us will taste death—all of us. Is there any greater victory for faith, or greater glorification to God than the willingness to *forego* God's protection in order to demonstrate the depth of faith? Placing ourselves voluntarily in harm's way, and willingly accepting the probability of danger to ourselves, for the sake of our faith in Christ, is one of faith's greatest victories.

Sometimes God is glorified by demonstrating His powerful protection over us, and sometimes God chooses to be glorified by our demonstration of a faith that can face down the greatest fear of all—death!

From the gallows we see that Mordecai was willing to forego God's protection, as he risked death through his actions.

With these valuable lessons from the gallows, we can draw some valuable practical applications that help to make sense of God's silence when we fully expect Him to speak up and act like God!

God Will Not Be Leashed

If we had our way, we would keep God on a short chain, close at hand so that we could unleash Him as soon as danger threatened. We would love for God to display His power and deliverance on command, but God resists that.

In C. S. Lewis's fantasy, *The Lion, The Witch, and the Wardrobe,* Mr. Beaver's description of Aslan, the great lion who represents Christ, is enlightening: "He doesn't like being tied down—and of course he has other countries to attend to. It's quite all right. He'll often drop in. Only you mustn't press him. He's wild you know. Not like a *tame* lion."[2] We do not have a God we can tame, He will not submit. He is sovereign and does not take direction.

From time to time my children get into disagreements and bickerings in our neighborhood, as all children do. Inevitably, they want me to come and enforce their will upon the other children, a task I perform reluctantly or not at all.

However, whenever they are in real danger, I am there in a flash. There are times when advice and counsel will suffice to help them solve their problems. There are also times when the danger is more real and only direct intervention will solve the problem. I know the difference; so does God.

Silence can be a speech

When God's personal revelation is enough to deal with our fear of danger, He often leaves it at that. When direct intervention is required, He knows that too.

Were it otherwise, our temptation would be to wear God like a gun, taking Him out and firing at whomever we felt was threatening us in any way. God righteously resists this type of involvement. Our judgment and assessment abilities

---

2. C. S. Lewis, *The Lion, The Witch, and the Wardrobe.* New York: Collier Books, 1970, 180.

are not fitted to that divine task. I shudder to think about the kind of destruction I would have visited upon innocent people if God had directly responded in the way I wanted toward those I had felt were a threat.

No, the silence of God is often testimony to the wisdom and righteousness of God *not* to intervene in the way we want. He alone has the ability to judge and act righteously and justly.

Our God cannot be leashed, and far from being disappointing, that should be a cause of celebration and relief. In silence we are often caused to reevaluate our own motivations, and frequently we find ourselves changing our minds. That silence, therefore, *was* the answer to our prayers.

As they said in the Old West, *"Silence can be a speech."*[3]

God Never Intended to Shield Us from the Perception of Danger

We often want to be protected not only from danger, but even the perception of it. There are no close calls with God. He's never had to breathe a sigh of relief at the culmination of a rescue. The outcome, for Him, was never in doubt.

But we don't want to have to face the pangs of fear, the anxiety attacks in the middle of the night, the shadow of loss or destruction looming over us.

We want God to simply keep the danger away from us in the first place, because trusting is such an agonizing and exhausting work. We want to be in great spiritual shape without ever having to exercise the muscles of faith.

3. Ken Alstad, *Savvy Sayings*. Tucson: Ken Alstad, 1986, 5.

Don't misunderstand me; God is intimately acquainted with and concerned with our feelings of fear and loss, whether they be perceptions of fear, or the real thing. He knows that we can't discern the difference from our vantage point.

For our real danger He has promised real protection, but for perception of danger, we are promised His presence to comfort and assure us that He is aware of our predicament and is on the case.

As a result of knowing that truth we can often conclude that if God hasn't yet intervened, we are not yet in the real danger we fear.

Learning to close the closets ourselves

When my children wake up in the middle of the night afraid of monsters in the dark, I do not protect them, for they aren't in any real danger. It is the perception of danger that grips their little hearts and minds. They aren't in need of rescue, but comfort. In those moments I allow them to climb in bed with me, and in a short time they are sound asleep, secure in the perception of safety.

My son used to be terribly afraid of the closet doors. When they were left open at night he would wake up and imagine all kinds of frightening possibilities. But while I comforted him in each case, I also taught him how to close the closet doors for himself before he went to sleep.

I think that sometimes the danger we feel is not real, but a closet we have left open in our lives that God wants us to learn to close for ourselves.

God hears the cry of His own

We must not forget that while Mordecai and Esther and the Jews called out for deliverance, so did Haman (7:7–8).

When we see the machinery designed for our destruction being erected around us, it can be a terrifying and intimidating experience. But, does it compare with Haman's last few moments? When his destruction was imminent, who could he call out to?

"God is our deliverer" is a statement that deserves more attention than it receives, especially if we consider the alternative.

While Mordecai's deliverance seemed to come slower than he might have wished—*it came!* Amid the hammering and construction of the gallows, God heard the cry of His people. Despite the power politicking occurring in Persia's powerful courts, God heard the cries of His people.

Haman's limp body, dangling seventy-five feet above the streets of Susa, screamed out the message: God hears the cry of His own!

Our eternal safety net

Without a single prophetic voice, or a single miraculous moment; without appearing in a burning bush or an earthquake, God proves again that He hears the cry of His own. It was the gallows that sent that message out to the world. It was the gallows that demonstrated the end of someone who had no god to deliver him. Haman proved the danger of being a spiritual orphan.

We have an eternal safety net, and that truth alone can empower us to face great danger, and take great risks. When we take a stand in our homes, offices, schools, and neighborhoods, and find ourselves out on a limb, pushed there by those who flaunt God and ridicule His power, we have the assurance of knowing that our cry will be heard.

When my children were very young, I saved them from countless perils they had no knowledge of: swimming pools, hot stoves, sharp-edged furniture, busy streets, large dogs, and myriad other dangers. I did this because they were mine. Every year millions of children suffer serious injuries, but I can't protect them, because I'm not there.

I make sure I am always there for my children. When my children are in danger, they know they have a daddy they can cry out to, who will protect them with his very life. God has already proven in Christ that He is willing to go that far.

God Becomes Deliverer to Us Only Through Great Danger

Most of the things we profess to believe about God are strictly hypothetical until tested. We casually repeat the words to the Lord's Prayer, *"deliver us from evil,"* but until we actually experience evil, we do not act as if God were our deliverer. Not until we are backed into a corner, completely out of ammunition, outnumbered, and surrounded, do we actually consider asking for deliverance.

It often takes a slow and growing sense of danger, and a recognition of our inadequacy to deal with it from our human resources, before we will consider and pray for the deliverance of God. It is not until the hypothetical is transformed into hope that God becomes real to us as our deliverer.

Have you addressed your critic within? What is it saying? Chances are it is questioning the character of a God who would allow the things that have happened to you to occur. You must address this critic. If you don't you will simply find his voice growing louder with each passing experience where God doesn't respond in the way you expect Him to. The more you try to silence this voice, the louder it will get.

Moses, David, Job, Elijah, Martha, and many other people of God voiced honest questions concerning the work of God in their lives. Each of them struggled with this inner critic.

We need to be honest; God's workings are at times mysterious and difficult to understand from our perspective, but thankfully, His nature is not, and therein lies one of the most powerful answers to the critic within.

God's eternal good-night kiss

My children often question my workings in their lives. When I withhold from them what they desire, or give to them what they least want, they get honestly frustrated. I'm sure at times they wonder just what kind of a man I am.

Because of the immaturity of their minds and experiences I could never explain to their satisfaction why I do some of the things I do. And because of the immaturity of our minds and experiences we can never be truly satisfied with some of God's actions in our lives.

However, my children don't have to exercise blind faith in me, for I have proven in countless ways that I love them dearly and am completely devoted to their well-being.

Several years ago, my daughter Christi made a Father's Day present for me. It is a treasured possession. It was simply a series of statements about me that she was supposed to fill in, in the form of a necktie. One sentence read: My favorite thing about my dad is: *"the way he always kisses me good-night."*

I don't think I ever understood how important that act was to her. It said at the end of every day, whether Daddy had done something she enjoyed, or something she didn't understand, that my love toward her was always constant. That kiss expressed my love, and my love helped silence the critic within her that would want to scream out, "Daddy doesn't love me; he's mean, and he doesn't care!"

Maybe that's why she wrote on another sentence: Daddy's favorite things are, *"Me, my mommy, Andrew, and Katie."* And maybe that's why I've hung that Father's Day present in my office where I could see it every day.

In a way, that's the favorite thing to me about my heavenly Father. In spite of all the things He allows in my life I don't understand, I know His heart's attitude toward me. God has displayed His love for me in so many ways, I cannot doubt it.

When God sent His Son to die for me, His only beloved Son, that was His eternal good-night kiss, proving once and for all His intentions toward me. Every experience I encounter will be correctly understood only in relation to that one event.

So don't be afraid to address the critic within when he points to one unexplainable experience or another. Just remind him of that incredible good-night kiss of God, and that of all His creation, *you* are His most precious possession.

Ironically, once we've honestly addressed the critic within, we are then able to see more clearly what was previously obscure. Doubt and dismay act as cataracts to our spiritual eyes, blinding us to God's greater purpose in our trials. When these cataracts are recognized and removed, we are often able to see more clearly what God was concerned with.

While our eyes could strain to see only our difficulty, God was focused on something else, as the end of Esther's story will show.

Eight

The Last Scene

A story is told of a farmer with three sons: Homer, Ted, and Ralph. No one in the family had ever attended church or had any time for God. The pastor and others in the church had tried for years to interest the family in the things of God, until one day Homer was bitten by a rattlesnake. The doctor was called in immediately and he did all he could to help Homer, but the outlook for his recovery was grim. As a last resort, the pastor was called in. The pastor finally arrived, took stock of the situation, and began to pray:

O wise and righteous Father, we thank You that in Your wisdom You sent this rattlesnake to bite Homer. Homer has never been inside the church and it is doubtful that he has, in all this time, ever prayed or even acknowledged Your existence. Now we hope that this experience will teach him a valuable lesson and will lead to his genuine repentance.

And now, O Father, will You send another rattlesnake to bite Ted, and another one to bite Ralph, and a really big one to bite the old man. Lord, You know that for years we have done everything we know to get them to turn to You, but with no success. It seems, therefore, that what we couldn't do with all our preaching, this rattlesnake has done. Therefore we can only conclude that the only thing that will do this family any real good is rattlesnakes, so, Lord, send us bigger and better rattlesnakes. Amen.

This crisis in Esther, the planned extermination of the Jewish nation by the wicked Haman, must have seemed like a rattlesnake bite to Mordecai and Esther, not the moving of the gracious hand of God.

I am here to tell you, however, from the truths of Scripture first, and my own experience second, that the longer you walk with God, the less you see life's incidents as rattlesnake bites, and the more you recognize them as the infinitely wise moving of a loving God.

You see, God is moving all of those who are His children to learn to follow His direction, until the last scene of our lives is played out. God has different priorities than we do. Our usual priority is to get through our next major problem or obstacle successfully. God's priority is to cause us to come to and grow in our faith in Him. Everything else is incidental to that goal. An event in life that may seem designed to destroy us, may seem like a rattlesnake bite, is in fact designed to strengthen and mature us.

In the last chapters of the book of Esther we are going to notice three principles of faith that jump out at us, demanding our attention.

Faith Is Measured by Patience

In Esther 9 we read,

In the twelfth month (that is, the month Adar), on the thirteenth day when the king's command and edict were about to be executed, on the day when the enemies of the Jews hoped to gain the mastery over them, it was turned to the contrary so that the Jews themselves gained the mastery over those who hated them. (9:1)

Now that seems to be a simple, straightforward statement, but how much is involved here? We need to keep in mind that the Jews had been informed of the decree to kill them almost a year earlier. Remember in chapter 4 when the Jews first heard of the decree? The decree was read and posted in every province in the Persian Empire, and there were Jews in many of these provinces. But interestingly, Haman, being superstitious, cast the lot (thrown dice) to determine when would be the most fortuitous time to carry out this horrible plan. It had fallen in the twelfth month, Adar, and the thirteenth day. But Haman had thrown the dice eleven months earlier. So the Jews had almost a year to wait, either for God's deliverance, or for death.

Living under the shadow

Now in chapter 8 we read that the king, after being made aware of Haman's plot, had two months later issued a new decree that allowed the Jews to defend themselves, but that's *all* the decree allowed. They had no idea how many would attack them, what their numbers would be like, what their chances were.

That would be something like being arrested for a murder you never committed, being sentenced to die by the courts, but being allowed to live your normal life in your own house for almost a year, until the execution date. At that time anyone who wanted to, by any means they desired to, were free to come and kill you and your wife and your children, *legally*. You lived literally under the shadow of death.

Finally, it was decreed that you had been given the right to defend yourself, but you still had no idea who was after you, how many there would be, or whether you would live or die. After the euphoria of learning you could fight back had worn off, you would have to face the grim task of preparing to fight to stay alive. What kind of a year do you think that would be for you? Sleep wouldn't be great, that's for sure. Long-term plans would be out.

Between hope and fear

They had to learn the difficult balance of living between hope and fear. We often encounter the same thing. One minute hope is strong as a rock in our God, and the next minute it can be as fragile as a flower's delicate petals. We teeter between these two extremes in life.

We forget the early lessons of our childhood. How many times did we fall down learning to walk? Yet we never considered blaming God for this blatant injustice. No, we have to grow up before we can reach that conclusion. Each fall got us one step closer to our goal of walking, and walking helped prepare us for running, then swimming, skating, and bicycling. Yet, it was a painfully slow process with far more failure than success.

They, like us, would probably be praying for an immediate deliverance. "God, save us, *quickly*." "Bring an end to this problem, *quickly*." "Don't let us stay in limbo so long."

We want to see the circumstances change, and God doesn't change them right away. The decree isn't nullified, rather, they are allowed to defend themselves, which actually drives them to trust Him further. They can smell deliverance but can't yet touch it. Furthermore, we find that is His pattern.

Second Corinthians 5:7 says, "We walk by faith, not by sight." And Hebrews 11:1–2 says, "Faith is the assurance of things hoped for, the conviction of things *not seen*. For by it the men of old gained approval" (italics added).

By what? By faith!

Hebrews 11:6 adds that "without faith it is impossible to please Him, for he who comes to God must believe that He is, and that He is a rewarder of those who seek Him."

Faith is measured by patience; but we want things to change quickly. We want deliverance quickly, we want answers quickly, we want to see progress *now*, we want to know how it's going to turn out *now*. And God often says, "No, wait, be patient, you need to learn to trust Me." How often we will say this to our children, and how often God has to say it to us. "No, wait, be patient, you need to learn to trust Me." Faith is measured by patience.

I once talked to a church group on the subject of "A Broken Home from a Child's Perspective." While I was years removed from the pain of that reality in my childhood, upon recalling it to them, I was surprised and embarrassed to find my voice cracking, being forced into silence for several moments before I could speak again.

This was terribly embarrassing to me, and I was feeling ashamed of myself. But after the class a woman who had attended wrote me a letter. She had grown up with a father who died of alcoholism when she was young. Accepting Christ when she was twenty, she thought she should immediately be able to get over all her pain. In her own words she wrote:

I know it was so very hard to share those personal hurts with all of us—but Dan, if you had not actually shown your pain, I would not have taken away from that lesson what I did. Seeing that you still feel pain from these times (and maybe personal experiences as well, in my case anyway)—showed me that it was OK to still hurt. It made me realize that God doesn't expect me to be over it all right now. Somehow I thought I didn't have enough faith to stop feeling the pain.

Faith is measured by patience, or more specifically, our faith is measured by our patience.

Faith, Not Results, Is the Goal of God

We see this second principle clearly in chapter 9. This chapter concerns the account of that day that the decree was to have been carried out for the destruction of the Jews. The decree's original intent was to destroy the people of God, but ironically (and providentially), it became the day on which their enemies were destroyed, and they were saved.

In fact, the Jews could never have foreseen that when the battle was to begin they would become the aggressors. Unknown to the Jews, the way God had brought down Haman and elevated Esther and Mordecai had quite literally put the fear of God into everyone. Instead of being bold and confident, their enemies became afraid. You see, originally they weren't expecting any kind of serious opposition. This was all supposed to be a walk in the park.

In the end we read that princes of the provinces, and many of the leaders in the Persian Empire, saw which way the wind was blowing and took the side of the Jews.

> Even all the princes of the provinces, the satraps, the governors, and those who were doing the king's business assisted the Jews, because the dread of Mordecai had fallen on them. (Esther 9:3)

Who could have foreseen that? No one, but God! In all, over seventy-five thousand of their enemies were killed on that day throughout the Persian Empire. Those people who had been so excited about destroying men, women, and children who had done them no harm found themselves victims of what they had been seeking to do.

Consider now the focus of the Jews and the focus of God during this whole process. The Jews were busy focusing on deliverance, victory, safety! Their main goal was to get out of this *alive*, to avoid destruction. God's main focus was on increasing their faith in Him. He alone knew there wasn't going to be a massacre of Jews. It was never meant to be. His focus was to reiterate through experience what He had reiterated before; He was to be trusted, in spite of the way things looked.

We also see that they learned a very important lesson. God did not deliver them so they could become rich off the plunder the king promised them they could have. The king's decree on behalf of the Jews stated they could plunder those they killed. But three times we are told explicitly they did *not* plunder (Esther 9:10–16).

God is not the candy man

They were learning. God did not deliver them so they could become rich, or have political clout through Esther and Mordecai. He delivered them to strengthen their faith, to increase their ability to trust in Him in spite of their apparent circumstances. Faith, not results, was God's goal. And it is the very same today. God wanted to take their eyes off the situation, the circumstances, and fix them on Him, His power, His ability to save, His sovereignty.

There is a lot of emphasis in certain Christian circles today on blessings. Searching for them, hoping for them, claiming them, strategizing to get them; and it is easy to focus on the results, and not on God's goal in all of it. God is not the candy man handing out treats to whoever will beg the best. He is the eternal God trying to get the attention of His people, saying, "My promises are more real and reliable then even what your eyes can see." Faith, not results, is the goal of God.

In the last part of chapter 9 and in chapter 10 we find one more principle of faith.

Faith Is Increased by Remembering

From Esther 9:20 to the end of chapter 10 we have recorded the actions of Mordecai and Esther, who actually create a national Jewish holiday. They name it the Feast of Purim, and it is still celebrated by some Jews today. It was to be a two-day feast because, while in some provinces the battle lasted only one day, in Susa they were given the approval to let the battle go on for two days. So it became mandatory that the Jews, every year, remember and celebrate the deliverance God gave to them over Haman.

The irony of the feast is in the name. The name *Purim* comes from the Persian word *pur*, meaning "lot." The Feast of Purim, or lots, refers to the fact that the eventual deliverance date of the Jews was determined by Haman himself, by his casting the *pur*, or dice. In Haman's mind, he was in control, and he set the date of destruction. In reality, God was in control, and He set that date as the date of deliverance. This feast has been celebrated for thousands of years.

Mordecai knew that faith is increased by remembering. How true that is! The more we keep track of what God has done for us, how He has gotten us out of jams, vindicated us, blessed us, the easier it is to trust Him in the next situation. The less we keep track of what God has done for us, the harder it is to trust Him in the next situation.

Write your own book

Probably the single greatest faith-building exercise you could devise would be to take a bulletin board and 3" x 5" cards, writing down and posting every instance where God answers a prayer. The more you post, the more you will realize what God is doing and how actively He is involved in your life. It makes you aware of His work on your behalf. Then, when God calls on you to take a difficult step, or to trust Him for something, you can get great confidence by just looking through your chronicle of God's faithfulness. When it comes to God's faithfulness, we all have short memories. We need to be reminded and reassured that God will be faithful again.

Several years ago, my wife, Annette, and I bought a book of blank pages. We call it our *Book of God's Faithfulness*. In it we have recorded ways God has been faithful to us, providing for us, caring for us, protecting us, and opening doors for us. Whenever God demonstrates His faithfulness, we write it in our book. One day we will fill it up, and our prayer is to then give a copy to each of our children, with a blank book of his or her own.

When faced with a great danger or obstacle, we can either fret and worry, or open the book and remember how God has worked on our behalf in the past. Our memory needs to be immersed in the acts of God's faithfulness.

Personal holy days

We have holidays to celebrate so many things, and so many of them have very little impact on us. But imagine for just a moment the effect that special holidays commemorating God's faithfulness in our lives would have on us. For example:

May 5—The day God provided that job I so desperately needed. It sure didn't look like I was going to get it, and we were down to our final resources. Things sure looked bleak. What a great day, what a great God! We'll never forget that . . .

September 2—We were in a terrible automobile accident, but all escaped with minor injuries. How close we came to death. We'll never forget it . . .

February 4—Today my cancer went into remission. To God be the glory, great things He has done! I'll never forget . . .

December 3—After so many years, God has proved His faithfulness in bringing along my spouse. We were married yesterday. How long I had prayed for this day, and how long it seemed that You weren't doing anything. Now I see what You were doing. I'll never forget this . . .

April 7—Today Mom turned the corner. She almost died, but God healed her and gave her back her life, and He gave us back ours. Can we ever thank You enough? We'll never forget . . .

June 30—Our first child was born today, healthy! There were many concerns about his physical condition, but God gave him complete health. What a time of anxiety we experienced over the last months. What a delivery! What a deliverance! What a Deliverer! We'll never forget this time . . .

Overcoming spiritual Alzheimer's

Let's admit it: anxiety attacks our memories first. We develop a spiritual Alzheimer's condition. When trouble hits we can't seem to remember any further back than the moment when our latest problem began.

And yet it is the very act of remembering that so strengthens our faith in God. Remembering God's past faithfulness doesn't remove our present problem, it puts it in perspective. It anesthetizes our panic.

I read a story not long ago about a mother who came down with a throat ailment. She was sure it was cancer. Evidently panicking, she began determining how her children would be cared for in her absence. In the end, panic overcame her, and sanity eluded her. She decided that her children would be better off with her in heaven than left behind. She then proceeded to shoot each of her children, finally turning the gun on herself. Ironically, an autopsy discovered she didn't have throat cancer after all.

Faith will either chase away fear, or fear will chase away faith.

Are you facing what seems like certain catastrophe? May I prescribe a dose of hope and perspective?

Get out a pen and paper and find a quiet place alone. There in the quietness of your own heart, tell God how honestly frightened and faithless you really are, and ask Him to help you remember past events where He delivered you. Then wait, quietly and patiently. When He helps you remember, write them down, and keep record of them. Don't be in a hurry; God may want to cause you to remember more than just one time.

If you are new in your faith, and you haven't had time to experience God's faithfulness firsthand, seek out a Christian friend you can trust. This exercise would be a wonderful opportunity for that person as well, increasing his or her faith as well as yours.

Faith is increased by remembering. We could do worse things than make special holidays of God's faithfulness to us.

Three timeless lessons, so easy to say, so hard to learn:

Faith is measured by patience.
Faith, not results, is the goal of God.
Faith is increased by remembering.

As we close the pages on the book of Esther, we cannot help but be encouraged that God is alive, and is in control in even the most minute events of our lives. He who stands in the shadows of our lives wants us to learn to trust Him, to follow His lead, and to recognize His presence.

The Unseen Player

There once was a family of mice who lived all their lives in a large piano. To them in their piano-world came the music of the instrument, filling all the dark spaces with sound and harmony. At first the mice were impressed by it. They drew comfort and wonder from the thought that there was Someone who made the music—though invisible to them—above, yet close to them. They loved to think of the Great Player whom they could not see.

Then one day a daring mouse climbed up part of the piano and returned very thoughtfully. He had found out how the music was made. Wires were the secret; tightly stretched wires of graduated lengths that trembled and vibrated. They must revise all their old beliefs; none but the most conservative could any longer believe in the Unseen Player.

Later, another explorer carried the explanation further. Hammers were now the secret, many hammers dancing and leaping on the wires. This was a more complicated theory, but it all went to show that they lived in a purely mechanical world. The Unseen Player came to be thought of as a myth. But the Pianist continued to play!

Can you hear the Pianist yet? Esther's drama ends, but the story may not be over, not yet. Though the stage has been cleared, the actors have all gone, the scenes and props have been removed, two yet remain in the theater.

One is the author, God; the other is you. This elaborate production was staged for you. His eyes are now on you, awaiting your reaction. Please don't leave quite yet.

Closing the Curtain

It's my day off today, and I'm writing these last words in the privacy of my home. It's a beautiful day with the wind blowing gently, the sun shining brightly, the blue sky comforting and reassuring.

As I look out my back window, I pause and watch a hummingbird, that amazing feathered flying miracle of God's creation, getting a drink from the feeder. Our hillside is blooming lavender, and vines are meandering up the posts of our redwood deck, with beautiful white blooms posing on their delicate limbs.

These words may sound strange after you have read this book, for this book deals with how God works in the crises of our lives. But they aren't really strange.

You see, there was a time when I would go an entire year and never appreciate the beauty around me. I never stopped, never listened, never looked. I was too busy worrying, too stressed out to notice or pay attention to anything other than the dark clouds of trouble in my life.

What a waste! I have learned that life happens: the good, the bad, and the ugly. I have also learned that I was too afraid to relax because in the deepest recesses of my heart, I feared that God really wasn't in control, or didn't care.

No more. I have learned that no matter how terrible a trial may come my way, no matter how hard it may hit, and no matter how unprepared I feel for it, God *is* in control! The sun will come out tomorrow morning, the birds will sing again, and I will survive! Why? Because God is most definitely in control of my life, and because He who is in control of this world, and my world, loves me *very much.*

How much this knowledge has changed my life! How desperately I hope it will change yours also!

Most of the words of this book have been admittedly directed to those faithful, but frustrated, Christians who struggle not with the existence of God, but with the activity of God, who are confused by His silence, unaware of His unceasing activity on their behalf. It is my sincere prayer that this book will turn on the lights, blow away some clouds of confusion, and help to heal a wounded heart.

But now the next step is yours, and yours alone. Our life is truly made up of choices, and what we choose to do with the truths we hear. We can know all the truths found in this book, even have them memorized, and yet still not change. In fact, a truth unclaimed can at times seem more like a curse, tantalizing us with a peace we do not as yet feel.

Confidence in God and His plan does not come from the gathering of information about Him, but rather the application of that knowledge. On a wall in my office is a piece of paper with the following words scribbled down. "The only truth you know is the truth you live, so don't take your knowledge too seriously." I wrote these words at a time in my life when I was weighed down with knowledge about God, but unable to gain any comfort from them, or see what practical difference they might make in my life.

Some truths about God sit on dusty shelves in our lives, unreached for, unused, but impressive to ourselves, and sometimes to others. They can foster false confidence. For it is one thing to concede intellectually that God is in control and that every act and movement on His part toward us is guided by His everlasting love; it is another matter to live as if that were true, to willingly accept what He brings, confident that it is for good, and not for evil. Until this truth, that God is in control, makes a difference in our lives, we have learned nothing.

But rest assured, God will press the issue; indeed, He must, for change is precisely what He is after. We are industrious about the changing of the outside, and soon after coming to Christ we learn to dress right, talk right, and look right, like little children playing dress up. But the essence of change, the fundamentally different way of looking at and reacting to life's difficulties, often eludes us.

In this moment, His eyes are on you. He knows the fear, the panic, the desperation you often feel when trouble comes. Yet, trouble, as we have seen in the book of Esther, must come—it is our tutor—to remind us of our Father's care and promise to conform us to the image of His son. Difficulties in life reveal not only where we are in our spiritual life, but where we need to go.

We believe too easily that if only circumstances were different, we would be different. We must let go of this false security blanket. Please believe me when I say that not one single thing has to change in your life to bring you peace. Not one situation requires alteration, not one tragedy requires removal.

On the contrary, if you can find peace in the knowledge that God is in control of your life, and intimately involved with it now, then God's peace is always going to be available to you. If things have to improve first, situations change, problems be removed, before you can rest in His providential care, this truth is simply academic, useless.

When I learned these truths in Esther I was going through some very difficult times. The difficulties didn't leave, they lingered for quite awhile, as real problems tend to do. The only thing that changed was me, and that was what God had in mind all along.

Until you have experienced it, you cannot imagine the joy of knowing peace in the midst of the storms of life, of knowing that fear and despair can never bully you again. Never is a truth more valuable than when it becomes more real to you than the trouble you face. And this is where He means to bring us.

It takes eyes of faith to see His shadow, but He has made this kind of insight available to you and me. I have seen His shadow, and I can recognize it now. I find it cast over every trial and blessing that comes my way. One day He will fill the shadow with His presence; when that happens, doubts and fears will no longer be possible. But until then, we'll just keep dancing, He and I.

Come dance with us.

Taking a Deeper Look

One: Dancing With a Shadow

1. Have you ever faced a crisis that seemed as if it would swallow you up? How did God move in the shadows to rescue you? What was happening behind the scenes that you weren't aware of?

2. What makes it so difficult to believe that God is really in control of the circumstances of life?

3. Have you ever experienced the "silence" of God in the midst of a crisis you were facing? Where did His silence ultimately lead in your life?

4. Try to recall two or three times when you "saw His shadow" in your own life—when God helped you in a way you could never have imagined.

5. God often uses crisis points, "scary rides," in our lives to cause us to trust in Him and His providential care for us. What situation in your life would you call a scary ride right now?

Action Step

Take a few moments and think of the looming crisis you are facing today. Be honest with God, telling Him that you've been worried, afraid you were on your own. Ask Him to reassure you of His presence in your life. Ask Him to help you realize how He is active, even when you can't see or feel Him at work.

Two: *Backstage Choreography*

1. Who are the powerful people in your world, and why do they seem so powerful to you?

2. In what way could God be using them as His powerful pawns in your life?

3. What are some of the things that people place their security in? How could those things be taken away?

4. What are the things *you* place your security in? Can these things be taken away or lost?

5. Try to think of an instance when God called you to do something, and you blew it. Were you faithful the next time? What made it difficult the first time?

6. God's faithfulness to us is not dependent upon our faithfulness to Him. Why is that sometimes so hard to believe? Do you struggle with believing this? If so, why?

7. Can you think of a time when God took your mistakes and failures and accomplished something positive with them?

8. What blessings or gifts has God given you? List at least five.

9. Do you remember a time when God requested that you unconditionally relinquish a blessing or gift He had given to you in trust? Was it difficult? Why?

10. Have you ever "hung yourself" (found yourself a victim of your own appetites) with an attitude or desire that was against God's will and plan? What warning signs did you ignore?

Action Step

In this chapter we saw that each character's life provided enough information to develop a epigram that describes the direction his or her life was taking.

> Ahasuerus: The powerful pawn of God.
> Vashti: The woman with a loose grip on security.
> Mordecai: Faithful the second time around.
> Esther: Person of privilege, person of responsibility.
> Haman: The man who hung himself.

Take some time and reflect on your own history, both past and present. Then write down a one line description of yourself and the direction you see your life taking.

Would you want this as your epitaph? Ask someone who knows you well whether or not they agree with the description you have given of yourself. Ask them what they would write, and why.

If your description is like Haman's or Ahasuerus', write a brief description of a new direction you would like your life to take, along with the specific changes you must implement to make this come true. Ask other Christians to pray with you that this new description would become a reality in your life.

Three: *Setting the Stage*

1. Take a pen and paper and write down one positive principle of living that you have chosen, and one negative principle you fell victim to. What were the results of both decisions?

2. "If we just plan well, work hard, don't quit, we will ultimately taste the success we're reaching for." Agree or Disagree? Why?

3. Do you find it difficult to give God the credit for your great successes? How much of your success do you feel you are responsible for, and how much is God responsible for?

4. Recount a time when your obedience to God came with a high price tag attached to it.

5. There are times when we are obedient to God, and the initial result is calamity instead of blessing, pressure instead of relief. Agree or Disagree? Why?

6. "What I am is more important than anything I can receive." In light of this principle, try to think of three words that best describe who you are.

7. I think if we were honest we'd all admit to wanting "a little bit more" to be satisfied with our lives. What "little bit more" will you admit to wanting?

8. "If you can't be content with what you have right now, you probably won't be content with anything. If you can be

content with what you have now, you can be content with more." Agree or Disagree? Why?

Action Step

Try to determine what ideas or principles guide your life. Be careful here; our natural tendency is to begin to think of Bible verses or pious platitudes that we feel *ought* to be influencing our lives, but they are not always what guide us.

No surface fishing will do here. Drop your line deep. Ask yourself, "When I'm faced with difficult decisions, what advice (or principle of living) do I rely on to help me along the way?" A close friend or spouse could help us here, as they see things that are often hidden from us.

After we feel we can articulate what this principle is, hold it up to scriptural scrutiny. Is this what you want to be driven by? Does this principle honor Christ and His Word? If not, retain what is good, but jettison everything else that will slow down your growth in godliness.

Four: Difficult Parts to Play

1. Think of one time God derailed your routine. How do you remember feeling when that happened? What was your immediate reaction?

2. There is a sign on an Alaskan highway that reads, "Pick your rut carefully, you'll be in it for the next 300 miles." Are you making any long-term commitments to your favorite ruts? What steps are you willing to take to prepare for any new path God may have for you?

3. Can you recall a time in your life when God asked you to walk by faith into the jaws of negative circumstances? Did you feel prepared?

4. Have you ever experienced the fact that doing the right thing in a difficult situation often seems to get harder, and not easier, as time goes on? Why do you think this is?

5. What are some difficult steps you are facing right now?

6. What is the price tag associated for doing the right thing?

Action Step

Confess to God that the part He has picked out for you to play right now is one you don't feel ready for. Begin to ask Him to strengthen your trust in Him so that you can be confident that the part He has picked out for you is one you are ready for, and you can act in spite of how you feel.

Five: *Struggling in Obscurity*

1. Can you think back over your life and point to one decision that you feel was so significant that you can measure your life by this one choice?

2. "The seeds of righteousness often take longer to bloom than we expect them to." Share one instance in your life where you cultivated godliness, but you did not instantly receive positive results.

3. Have you planted seeds of righteousness in the past that you can begin to cultivate now?

4. "Surely God will see, surely He will act." Have you ever thought this after planting a seed of righteousness? What kind of time table for growth did you have in mind when you planted your seed of righteousness?

5. What "deceptive weeds" have grown where you planted righteousness in your life or in the life of someone you love?

6. "While we're busy planting seeds of righteousness in our lives, Satan is just as busy planting weeds of righteousness around our lives." Agree or Disagree? Why?

7. Have you ever seen righteousness sprout late, long after you had planted the seed? What did you learn from the delay?

8. If we're honest we'll admit we all plant some weed seeds rather thoughtlessly in our lives. What weed seeds can you identify in your own life?

9. Is there a seed of righteousness you have planted that seems late in blooming? What is it?

Action Step

Let's stop and take stock of exactly what we're planting in our lives, both seeds of righteousness and weeds of unrighteousness. Weeds need little attention, and they grow rapidly, while seeds of righteousness need much greater care.

Make a list of the weeds you've been inadvertently planting in your life. Ask God to make you aware of all of them. Then list the seeds of righteousness you'd like to replace them with.

Find a small group of godly men or women who will hold you accountable to cultivating a new harvest in your life.

Six: *When the Spotlight Hits*

1. What is your greatest "I don't know" question right now? What decision or choice concerns you most?

2. Does an "I don't know" question in your life tend to cause you to lean on God more, or less? Why?

3. List two or three important ways you believe God has worked in your past that help to guide future decisions.

4. What position has God placed you in today that you feel is important to present and future decisions?

5. Where have you been positioned to have a significant impact on others for Christ? What is your platform?

6. Do you ever recall making a significant decision while "flying blind?" What was the result?

7. Who would you consider to be your mentors?

8. "God often reveals the next move, without revealing the final solution." Agree or Disagree?

Action Step

Take your greatest "I don't know" and consider these four factors: 1. The knowledge of how God has worked in your past, 2. The position God has placed you in today, 3. The truths God has already revealed, and 4. The example of godly mentors. Ask God to guide your decision-making process and then decide! Don't put it off anymore.

Seven: *Answering the Critics*

1. Have you ever had a cherished spiritual belief suddenly challenged by catastrophe? What was it, and how did it get challenged?

2. "More than one Christian has stumbled because they failed to adequately address the critic within." What emotions did you encounter when your "inner critic" raised its voice against God or His working in your life?

3. Can you point to any examples of "God's billboards"—occasions when God used highly visible situations to silently show His power or sovereignty.

4. "God wants us to know the extent to which He can protect us." Agree or Disagree? Why?

5. Have you ever "placed yourself in harm's way" for the sake of your faith in Christ? If so, how?

6. Have you ever found yourself praying for God to enforce your will on someone else? What helped you to discover that this was happening?

7. Are there doors on any "closets of fear" you think God wants to teach you to close? Would you share one?

8. "We have an eternal safety net." In what way could this truth give us courage?

9. Are you aware of any "hypothetical beliefs" you have about God that are yet to be tested in your life?

10. How could the "good-night kiss" of God help to silence the critic within us?

Action Step

Each of us has unanswered questions and unstated criticism regarding God's working in our world or our own personal lives. (And if we don't now, we soon will!) We are often tempted to ignore these, believing that dealing with them is an admission of doubt, and a sign of a lack of faith. But the truth is that each of us has doubts—even John the Baptist had doubts about Jesus at one point. Furthermore, if a doubt exists in us, it won't go away until we deal with it. The only thing it can do is grow.

Take some time and try to determine if there are any questions or criticisms of God that are lurking in your life. Bring them out in the open and write them down. Don't be afraid of them. God isn't! If you can't find a quick answer, don't panic, some questions take more time to understand than others. Scripture and godly mentors are excellent resources, but in that order. Begin to address the critic within yourself.

Eight: *The Last Scene*

1. Describe a rattlesnake bite that you have experienced—an event that seemed designed to destroy you.

2. Can you find any good that came out of that rattlesnake bite?
   - ❏ No, none at all.
   - ❏ Very little, it happened too recently.
   - ❏ A little, but I'm seeing more all the time.
   - ❏ A lot! (Share it.)

3. Have you ever been frustrated with God because He has allowed you to be "in limbo" (not knowing the outcome about a particular trial or issue) for so long?

4. Is there an issue in your life right now in which God seems to be telling you, "Wait, be patient, you need to learn to trust Me." What lessons do you think God is trying to teach you about Himself?

5. If faith is measured by patience, my faith on a scale of 1–10 would rate _____.

6. What do you think God would most like to teach you about Himself, even though you are too busy trying to get out of the problem to learn?

7. Take a few moments and recall instances in which God has gotten you out of jams, blessed you, or vindicated you.

8. Think of one special instance in which God's answered a special prayer for you, and give it a "Holiday" name.

9. "When trouble hits, we can't seem to remember any further back than the moment our latest problem began." Is this true in your life? Why?

Action Step

Get a set of 3-by-5 cards or a blank book and begin journaling every time God answers a prayer, gets you out of a jam, blesses you, or vindicates you. Review these when you need to remember how much God cares for every area of your life.

Get a calendar and begin keeping track of some of the most noteworthy instances, creating your own special "family holidays," to celebrate His work for you.

Closing the Curtain

1. The most prominent emotion I am feeling at this time is . . . . It is the result of . . . .

2. The last time I was really able to relax and enjoy myself, free from worry was . . . .

3. The truths I have learned in this book are
   ❏ All new to me.
   ❏ Mostly new to me.
   ❏ Mostly familiar, but some are new.
   ❏ All are familiar, none are new.

4. "The only truths you know are the truths you live." Agree or disagree? Why?

5. Finish this sentence: The greatest thing I have learned about the silence of God is that . . . .

6. "The only thing that changed was me, and that's what He had in mind all the time." What changes do you think God wants to make in you as you consider your own difficulties and trials?

Action Step

It was stated in the final chapter that "never is a truth more valuable then when it becomes more real to you than the trouble you face." In this final action step, I urge you to write a letter to God. In this letter, simply share honestly and simply what trouble is most on your mind, causing you the greatest distress. Then write down the truth you have learned from Esther that needs to become more real to you.

Tell God that you wish to appropriate the eyes of faith He wants to make available to you, so that the truth would become more real to you than the trouble. Tell Him that you are seeking the rest He gives for your heart and life.

Tell Him finally that you wish to be able to see His shadow, to recognize it and be reassured by it in your life. Put this letter in your Bible, or somewhere private, and each time fears about situations well up inside you and threaten to overwhelm you, pull the letter out and repeat your desire to God. Make it your prayer.

Note to the Reader

The publisher invites you to share your response to the message of this book by writing Discovery House Publishers, P. O. Box 3566, Grand Rapids, MI 49501, U.S.A. or by calling 1-800-653-8333. For information about other Discovery House publications, contact us at the same address and phone number.